Rubber Stamping
for the first time

Rubber Stamping
for the first time

Carol Scheffler

Sterling Publishing Co., Inc.
New York
A Sterling/Chapelle Book

Chapelle Ltd.

Owner: Jo Packham

Design/layout Editor: Leslie Ridenour

Staff: Marie Barber, Ann Bear, Areta Bingham, Kass Burchett, Rebecca Christensen, Dana Durney, Holly Fuller, Marilyn Goff, Holly Hollingsworth, Susan Jorgensen, Barbara Milburn, Linda Orton, Karmen Quinney, Cindy Stoeckl

If you have any questions or comments, please contact: Chapelle Ltd., Inc. P.O. Box 9252 Ogden, UT 84409 Phone: (801) 621-2777 FAX: (801) 621-2788 e-mail: Chapelle1@aol.com

Library of Congress Cataloging-in-Publication Data Available

10   9   8   7   6   5   4   3   2   1

A Sterling/Chapelle Book

Published in paperback 2004 by
Sterling Publishing Co., Inc.
387 Park Avenue South, New York, NY 10016
© 1999 by Chapelle Ltd.
Distributed in Canada by Sterling Publishing
% Canadian Manda Group, One Atlantic Avenue, Suite 105
Toronto, Ontario, Canada M6K 3E7
Distributed in Great Britain by Chrysalis Books
64 Brewery Road, London N7 9NT, England
Distributed in Australia by Capricorn Link (Australia) Pty Ltd.
P.O. Box 704, Windsor, NSW 2756, Australia

Printed in China
All Rights Reserved

Sterling ISBN 0-8069-5945-2 (hardcover)
1-4027-1360-6 (paperback)

Acknowledgements

Writing this book has been a true pleasure, made even more joyful by my association with some wonderful people. To all of them, I extend my heartfelt thanks. . . .

To Jo Packham and Lincoln Boehm and their dedicated staffs at Chapelle, Ltd., and Sterling Publishing Co., Inc.—for your discerning taste, commitment to quality, and thoughtful guidance every step of the way.

To Susan Lewen, Kristen Powers, the folks at The Paper Garden, Effie Glitzfinger, Printworks, and my dear friends at Great American Stamp Store—for your generosity, talent, and kind support!

To Katie Couric, Matt Lauer, and Ann Curry—for sharing my enthusiasm for crafts each month on the TODAY SHOW.

To Amy Wasserstrom, Cheryl Wells, Linda Finnell, and Jeff Zucker—for your commitment to nurturing the creative spirit of the TODAY SHOW's audience.

And, finally, to my parents, Bobbi and Jim Reich, and sister and brother-in-law, Amy and Ira Kaplan—for being my earliest and most constant fans and supporters; and my in-laws, Morris and Ann Scheffler—for being great baby-sitters and cheerleaders.

joys of porcelain painting, velvet embossing, candle making, decoupage, unique gift wrapping, broken plate mosaics, memory albums, and creating family keepsakes, to name a few.

In Carol's very first TODAY SHOW segment, she shared the wonders of rubber stamping with Katie Couric. Carol's passion for rubber stamping began over ten years ago. Since that time, her own stamp collection has grown wildly out of control and there is no end in sight. She has taught rubber stamping for many years and contributes to a number of journals, including Rubber Stamper, Stamper's Sampler, and Vamp Stamp News. Carol currently demonstrates rubber stamping on the popular public television program, Hands on Crafts for Kids, as its guest expert.

Carol writes about the hottest crafting tips and trends on TODAY.MSNBC.com. She also contributes to a variety of crafts magazines and is sought out often as an arts and crafts expert by newspapers across the U.S. Carol is in high demand as a teacher and guest demonstrator/speaker at craft stores, schools, and charitable events.

Carol attributes her ease in front of the camera to the years she spent as a professional actress. A graduate of Northwestern University's prestigious Theater Arts Department, she worked extensively in both regional and off-Broadway theater. She is proud to have been a featured actress at the Actors Theater of Louisville the year it won the Tony award.

Between stamping projects, Carol manages to find time to spend with her husband, Michael, and their three daughters, Madeline (12), Eliza (8), and Susannah (5). They reside in Larchmont, New York.

About the Author

Carol Scheffler is the Arts and Crafts Contributor to NBC's TODAY SHOW. She presents innovative and exciting craft ideas to the show's millions of viewers in the United States and around the world. Each segment features a different craft, showcasing the diversity and depth of Carol's talents. Carol has introduced the TODAY SHOW audience to the

Dedication

To Madeline, Eliza, and Susannah—you've endured a lot of take-out dinners and "Not now, Mommy's working" with great patience and loving support.

To Michael—you thought this was going to be my project?! Surprise! "Thanks" seems too small a word. I love you.

contents

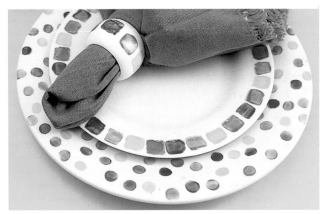

Rubber stamping for the first time

Welcome to the world of rubber stamping! I am delighted to introduce you to what I promise will become a fulfilling and exciting hobby. You will be making cards, gifts, decorative items for your home, and a host of other projects that will look terrific and give you a great sense of accomplishment. And the best part is, you can start right now!

When I look back over my own early experiences with this craft, I realize that the initial attraction for me was that I could create beautiful projects without having to draw. Someone else has done the drawing for you. You have the fun of taking their image and making it come to life through the magic of rubber stamping.

You will be amazed by the variety of images available. There are thousands of rubber stamps to suit every imaginable style. Everything from adorable to elegant, primitive to victorian, abstract to realistic—the choices are endless. As you become comfortable with the craft and gain confidence as a stamper, your own style will develop naturally, but I recommend that you continue to experiment with all different sorts of images and stamping techniques. Stretching yourself in your craft keeps it interesting and gives you a chance to discover new sides of your creative self.

An undeniable appeal of this craft is the fact that you can complete a great looking project in minutes. You don't need to survive a three month course or struggle through labor intensive projects, only to be disappointed with the results. My guess is that by tonight you will have created a project that you will be proud of.

Stamped artwork comes together quickly. Many of the projects in this book can be made in 10 minutes or less. Even most of the advanced projects will take you less than an hour. If you are like me, craft projects are accomplished in stolen moments, between paying bills and driving carpool. A fast project is a real plus!

With all the crafting I do for NBC's TODAY SHOW, magazines, books, and teaching, rubber stamping is the craft I always return to. In trying to figure out why, I come up with one overriding reason. Versatility. Rubber stamping can be used on practically every project I want to tackle— making a memory book, crafting a new lamp shade for the bedroom, designing a sweatshirt for one of my daughters, or creating a special birthday card for a friend. With rubber stamps, I can achieve so many different looks, all with professional polish.

But be forewarned—rubber stamping is addictive. You will start to play with your stamps and lose track of time and the next thing you know, it is 2:00 a.m. But the creative satisfaction and the chance to forget about "real life" and become totally engrossed in a project is worth a little sleep deprivation!

So, once again, welcome and thank you for joining me on this creative journey through the world of rubber stamping.

Carol Scheffler

How to use this book . . .

I have written this book for the beginning rubber stamp artist. The first section of the book familiarizes you with the various tools and materials you will need to get started. The second section introduces basic techniques that will serve as the building blocks for all your stamped artwork. Each project introduces a new technique. If you decide to jump ahead to a project out of sequence, you may find you have skipped a project which introduced a technique you now need to use. Check the Table of Contents or the index to find the information you need. In addition to the techniques, I have included some design ideas and troubleshooting tips to help you create a piece that will make you proud to say, "I made it myself."

While I provide information that will allow you to make the projects exactly as they are pictured, you should feel free to alter any or all of the specific elements of the design in a way that appeals to you. My projects are only meant to serve as examples to illustrate the technique I am describing. If you like the idea of a bookmark, but want to use fish stamps in greens and blues instead of the raspberry stamp I colored with magenta and red, by all means, make the substitution. That is the beauty of rubber stamping—you are the designer.

In the third section of the book we go beyond the basics, using stamps on a variety of surfaces and in unconventional ways. I will provide you with the information and tools you need to accomplish your goals. You will see that these projects are not more difficult; they just require some adjustments in the techniques we learned in Section Two. Soon, you will be stamping on every surface in sight, creating beautifully designed pieces!

What can be achieved with rubber stamps is only limited by one's imagination, so in Section Four, I provide you with inspiration for your imagination by showcasing the work of some of today's top stamp designers and stamping artists. Don't be intimidated by what you see. You will have learned all the basic techniques that are required to make these projects. It is time to play, combine techniques, break rules, and color outside the lines. You will be delighted with what you discover.

section 1: *rubber stamp basics*

What do I need to get started?

Basic Materials

For the most basic rubber stamp project, you will need just a few tools.

1. Brush art markers in a variety of colors, dye-based ink pads in rainbow and/or solid colors, paper, and rubber stamps (acrylic mounted, foam mounted, or wood mounted).

To create more sophisticated projects, you will also need the following tools.

2. A craft knife, a cutting mat, decorative-edged scissors, and a ruler.

3. A bone folder, card stock in a variety of colors, paper in a variety of patterns, and paper adhesive (double-sided tape, dry bond, or paper glue).

4. Dual-tipped brush art markers in a variety of colors, colored pencils, and a black permanent ink pad (not shown).

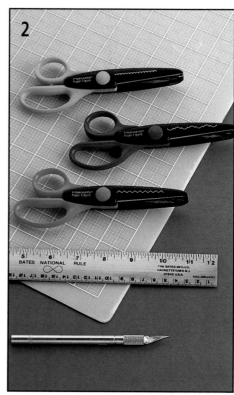

Materials to Create Special Effects

To accomplish the following special effects, you should also purchase the following materials.

1. *To heat-emboss* — pigment ink pads (rainbow and/or solids), a heat gun, and embossing powder (clear, metallic, colored, or specialty).

2. *To layer paper* — a paper cutter (with or without a variety of cutting blades), decorative-edged scissors, hole and shape punches, and textured and handmade papers.

3. *To give a soft-colored effect* — a sponge, watercolor pencils, chalks, and a watercolor paint set.

4. *To embellish your artwork* — brass charms, raffia, buttons or whatever inspires you!

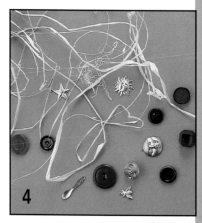

5. *To add sparkle* — ultrafine glitter, double-sided tape, a glue marker or pen (not a glue stick), sparkle glue in a squeeze bottle, and glittery adhesive-backed paper (not shown).

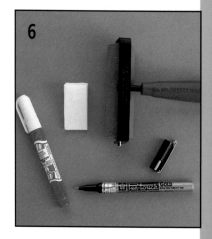

6. *To create interesting backgrounds* — a rubber brayer, a sponge brayer (not shown), wedge-shaped makeup sponges, round utility sponges (not shown), patterned papers (not shown), metallic markers, a white correction pen . . . experiment with other tools that you find!

7. *To create dimension* — adhesive foam tape or dots, corrugated cardboard, a paper crimper, and dimensional paints.

8. *To stamp on fabric* — fabric paint (not shown), bold-faced fabric stamps (not shown), sponge brushes, cotton swabs, fabric ink pads, fabric markers, and your fabric item.

What will it cost me to get started?

One of the wonderful things about rubber stamping is that getting started does not require a large investment of money. Average-sized, wood-mounted stamps cost between $4.00–$8.00. Foam-mounted sets of five to eight stamps cost about $10.00. Dye-based ink pads cost about $4.50. A prepackaged set of 10 cards and envelopes costs about $5.00. A package of 12 brush art markers costs about $18.00.

How do I set up my work space?

Always stamp on a stack of scrap paper or newsprint. The soft padding of the paper helps you achieve a better impression when you print the image. The paper will protect the work surface from possible ink smears and is also a good place to try out a stamp to help you decide whether to incorporate it into your work.

Have a damp paper towel sitting on a plastic plate nearby to wipe off the excess ink on the stamp once you have finished using it. You may also want to have handy a dry paper towel or cloth towel to dry off the stamp once you have cleaned it.

If you are using markers, store them standing with the tips down in a mug or similar container so that they don't roll away from you. Gather the stamps you have chosen and the paper and . . . begin!

How do I clean my stamps?

Most ink will clean off stamps easily with a damp paper towel. Pigment ink may need a little scrubbing with an old toothbrush to come completely clean. Stubborn ink can be treated with a small amount of window cleaner diluted in water. Avoid submerging the stamp in water or else the glue holding everything together will start to dissolve. Permanent inks must be cleaned off with a solvent cleaner made for this purpose.

How do I store my materials?

All ink pads and markers are best stored upside down. This keeps the ink on the top of the pad or marker tip where you need it. Papers should be stored flat and in a place where they will be kept clean. Keep all stamping materials out of direct sunlight and away from dust.

Stamps should be clean and dry when you put them away. They should be stored flat, rubber die side down.

15

What are the different parts of a stamp?

All stamps consist of a piece of rubber into which an image has been impressed (known as a die), a piece of foam cushion, and a mount. The mount is the handle, so to speak, with a picture of the image (the index) glued or printed on top of it. Mounts can be made of wood, foam, or acrylic block.

1. *Wood-mounted stamps* — These stamps are a bit more expensive, but many stamping artists like the sturdy feel of the wood.

2. *Foam-mounted stamps* — These stamps are much less expensive, but stamp very nicely.

3. *Acrylic-mounted stamps* — These are transparent, allowing the stamping artist to see exactly where the image is being printed. There are not many stamps available with acrylic block mounts and they can be as expensive as wood-mounted stamps.

Some stamps are also mounted onto a wheel (not shown), allowing for a continuous printing of an image as you roll it along.

What are the basic kinds of stamps?

There are basically three kinds of stamps: bold-faced, highly detailed, and outline. Each one has its own look and requires a different approach to inking. While there are no hard and fast rules, I have provided some guidelines as to which inking techniques will consistently produce the best results. However, I encourage you to experiment on your own and develop a sense of what appeals to you.

1. *Bold-faced stamps* — A bold-faced stamp has a wide expanse of raised rubber. Detail is usually minimal. These stamps can be inked with a single color, but they look wonderful when colored with a few different brush art markers, or inked with a rainbow pad. Try inking a bold-faced stamp with a pigment pad or pigment ink markers. Then print and heat-emboss the image—the bold image looks very dramatic when it is raised and shiny.

2. *Highly detailed stamps* — These stamps have a great amount of detail in the rubber die. Images may have a lot of stippling or fine lines incorporated into them to provide realistic detail. Printing a highly detailed image is best achieved by using a dark-colored ink. Heat-embossing these printed images works best if you use a very fine embossing powder called a "detail embossing powder."

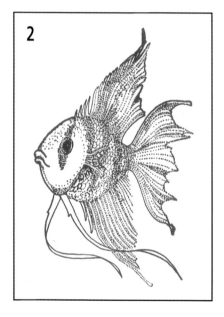

3. *Outline stamps* — Outline stamps, also known as cartoon stamps, are simple outlines of images without much detail. They work well when the outline is printed and then the interior is colored in with markers, pencils, or paints. Outline stamps work well when the printed image is heat-embossed.

How do I choose the right paper?

There is a seemingly infinite variety of paper available to the stamp artist and choosing the right paper can seem tricky. Each paper has its own qualities which make it more or less appropriate for a certain project.

If you want your artwork to last for generations, make certain your paper is acid free, archival, or pH neutral. Papers made without these specifications can yellow, become brittle, and fade over time. Archival quality papers and card stocks are readily available in craft and rubber stamp stores.

Here is a guide to help you in your paper selection:

1. *Card stock paper* — This is the paper you will select most often. It is a smooth, heavy-weight paper that comes in a wide variety of colors and patterns and is also available in matte (not shiny) and glossy finishes. Glossy-finish card stock is exciting for stamping artists to use because it makes colors look vibrant. It can be a little slippery to stamp on and may take a little getting used to.

Stamping with pigment inks on glossy card stock requires heat-embossing to permanently set the ink. If pigment ink is not heat-embossed on glossy card stock, it will not dry and, consequently, will smear.

Card stock takes ink beautifully and has a substantial feel to it, giving your work a professional look. Usually it is sold in 8½" x 11" sheets. You should purchase a variety of colors for constructing your own cards and for use in paper layering.

You will also find prepackaged folded cards with envelopes in craft and rubber stamp stores. They are a great choice for the beginner because they come in a variety of sizes and colors and are ready to use.

2. *Text-weight paper* — This is a lightweight paper that is most similar in weight to computer paper. It is available in a wide variety of colors and patterns. You can adhere it to the top of card stock as an embellishment or use it to make your own stationery.

3. *Cover-weight paper*— This is slightly heavier and thicker than text-weight paper and is a great choice for stationery.

4. *Fancy paper* — Marbleized papers; corrugated papers; metallic crinkled papers; handmade papers with flowers, seeds, and leaves embedded in them; papers made of tree barks; thin papers with gold threads running through them . . . the selection is dazzling. These papers all make wonderful layering additions to your cards, but generally do not provide a suitable surface for stamping.

5. *Tissue paper* — Tissue paper is available in a variety of colors and patterns. This paper makes a fun stamping surface, although it is somewhat fragile. Dye-based inks work best on this thin paper.

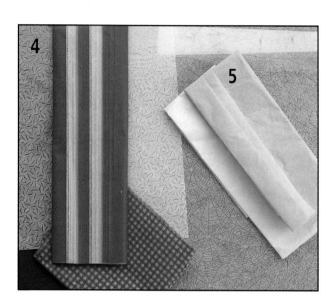

6. *Vellum paper* — Vellum is a very smooth, translucent paper. It comes in both text weight and card stock weight. The text-weight vellum makes an elegant liner inside a card. The card stock weight is fun to heat-emboss and layer over a printed card. Because you can see through it, the play between the two layers can produce interesting effects. Vellum paper, like glossy card stock, is coated so that the ink sits on top of the paper instead of soaking into it. What this means for the stamp artist is that if you use pigment ink on vellum, it must be heat-embossed to become permanent. If not heat-embossed, pigment ink on vellum will smear.

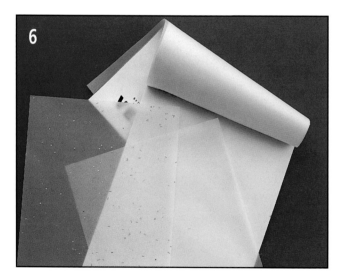

7. *Sticker paper* — Sticker paper comes in both matte and glossy formats. It is generally a white paper with an adhesive backing. You will have fun using it to apply stamped images to your artwork. Sticker paper is not a good surface on which to heat-emboss because the heat gun will cause the adhesive on the back of the paper to buckle.

8. *Construction paper* — I do not recommend construction paper (not shown) for rubber stamp projects. It is an inexpensive paper that does not hold up well to stamping, paper layering, or the test of time. It fades quickly and rips easily.

How do I choose the right ink?

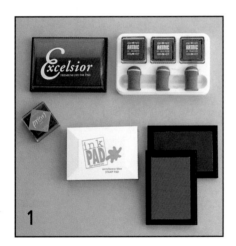

It is important to recognize that one ink or ink pad may not necessarily be the same as another. Different types of ink have been specially formulated for specific surfaces and effects.

1. *Dye-based ink* — Dye-based ink is a thinner ink and works especially well on a detailed stamp. It is available in ink pads and brush art markers. With dye-based ink pads, the ink is saturated onto a felt pad and encased in plastic. They come in different sizes and a wide variety of colors, as well as rainbow pad format. Re-inkers are available for dye-based ink pads when they begin to dry out. The colors will mix with each other if they come into contact on very absorbent paper, which is an effect you may or may not be trying to achieve. This ink dries quickly, is not formulated for heat-embossing, and will fade over time. Because the ink is water-based, it cleans up easily with water.

2. *Pigment ink* — Pigment inks are a thicker ink, formulated to stay separate on the paper and not mix with other colors. It is also a much slower drying ink than dye-based ink. This makes pigment ink perfect for heat-embossing. Pigment ink will dry on uncoated papers, but can take several minutes or up to several hours. Unless it is heat-embossed, pigment ink will not dry on coated papers, such as glossy card stock. Pigment ink is available in two formats—markers and pads. The pads are available in a variety of sizes and consist of a saturated foam pad encased in plastic. Pigment ink pads are available in a wide variety of colors and metallics, as well as rainbow colors and even clear. Re-inkers are available for pads that have become dry. Pigment ink will resist fading over time.

3. *Permanent ink* — Permanent ink is just that, permanent. It requires a solvent-based cleaner for cleaning. Permanent ink pads come in a limited number of colors. I highly recommend using black permanent ink with detailed stamps and outline stamps. When you color the printed images with water-based markers, you will not drag the black outline into the colored markers as you would if the outlines were stamped with a dye-based ink pad or marker.

4. *Fabric ink* — Fabric inks are formulated to be permanent on fabric, even when washed. The ink is saturated onto foam pads encased in plastic. They are available in a wide variety of colors. Re-inkers are also available.

5. *Crafter's ink* — Crafter's ink is a multipurpose pigment ink, formulated to be permanent when heat set. It is suitable for use on wood, fabric, shrink plastic, and terra-cotta. It is available in rainbow pads in which each individual color is removable from the entire collection of pads, if desired. The ink is saturated onto a foam pad and encased in plastic.

How do I stamp on other surfaces?

When you first became interested in rubber stamping, you probably envisioned yourself creating projects on paper. That is the logical place to begin. As you become more familiar with the basic techniques, you will look for other materials on which to stamp and discover that the choices are plentiful! Basically, you can print an image on any surface your heart desires, as long as you use the correct ink. Fabric, plastic, terra-cotta, wood, cork, metal, walls, porcelain . . . the list is seemingly endless. You will soon be stamping on all these surfaces and more and get terrific results, but it is a good idea to start with paper. As the song goes, "let's start at the very beginning . . . ."

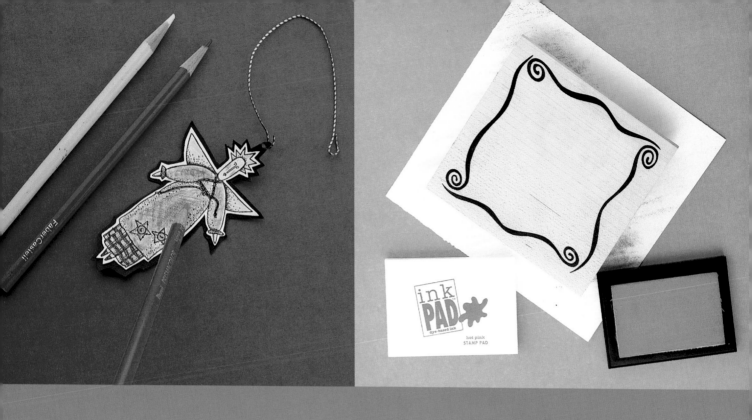

section 2: *techniques*

How do I ink a stamp with a marker?

What You Need to Get Started:

Brush art marker:
    magenta
Folded gift tag:
    glossy white
    (cut to size to fit
    your stamp)
Hole punch: ⅛"
Ribbon: satin,
    ⅛"-wide,
    magenta (8")
Stamp: girl
    holding a heart

When you think of inking rubber stamps, you probably think of ink pads. Ink pads are a good choice for doing the job, but did you know that you can also ink a stamp with a colored brush art marker? They work beautifully and give you a tremendous array of color choices for a very small investment. And, it couldn't be easier!

Simple Gift Tag

Here's How:

1. Ink the stamp, using the magenta marker and the following method:

- Hold the stamp, rubber die side up, in one hand.

- Hold the marker in your other hand and brush it against the rubber die, using the side of the marker, not the tip. This helps achieve quick coverage without wearing down the tip of your marker.

- Color the entire image. Remember, the part of the rubber die that makes the impression is the raised part. The recessed part of the image does not print and, therefore, should not be colored.

2. Give a quick puff of your breath on the image to remoisten the ink.

3. Print the image by placing the stamp, rubber die side down, onto the front of the gift tag. Without rocking or twisting the stamp, give it a little pressure. It does not take a lot of muscle.

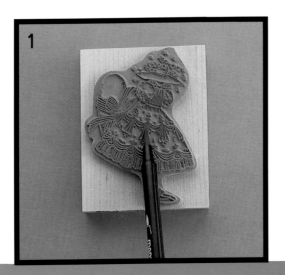

4. Lift the stamp straight up and off the gift tag. Admire your work!

5. Using the hole punch, punch a hole in the upper left-hand corner of the gift tag.

6. Thread the ribbon through the hole.

How to Thread a Gift Tag Ribbon:

1. Fold the ribbon in half.

2. Insert the folded end of the ribbon through the punched hole and pull through about 2".

3. Using your fingers, open up the folded end to form a loop.

4. Thread the two loose ends of the ribbon through the loop you are holding.

5. Pull the loose ends gently so that the loop tightens around the card corner.

2

What are the different methods I can use for coloring a stamped image?

What You Need to Get Started:

Card stock: dark
    green; white
Chalk eraser
Chalks: forest
    green; red; tan;
    yellow
Colored pencils:
    forest green;
    red; tan; yellow
Cup of water
Dual-tipped brush
    art markers:
    forest green;
    red; tan; yellow
Hole punch: ¹⁄₁₆"
Makeup
    applicator:
    sponge-tipped
Paintbrushes:
    flat; liner
Paper adhesive
Paper cord: green
    and gold
Pencil sharpener
Permanent ink
    pad: black
Scissors
Spray acrylic
    sealer: matte
    finish (to
    set chalk)
Stamp: folk art
    angel
Watercolor
    paints: forest
    green; red; tan;
    yellow

There are many different tools you can use to color a stamped image, each producing a different effect. Dual-tipped brush art markers produce a bold-looking image whereas colored pencils or watercolor paints produce a softer glow. Watercolors and chalks are easy to mix and a natural choice for shading. Different pencil colors can be layered and intermingled, adding depth to your work. Take some time to play with these coloring tools and discover the effects you can achieve. Experimentation will produce exciting results!

Angel Ornaments

Here's How:
1. Ink the stamp, using the black ink pad. Print the image four times onto white card stock.

2. Using scissors, cut out each stamped image, leaving ¼" of white card stock all around the edge.

3. Apply adhesive to the back of each stamped image and adhere them onto dark green card stock.

4. Using the scissors, cut the dark green card stock around each image, leaving a ¼" border all the way around, except at the top of the angel's crown, leaving enough paper to punch a hole for the cord.

5. Refer to pages 27–28. Color the stamped image with either chalks, colored pencils, markers, or watercolor paints, following the specific instructions for each coloring technique.

6. Using the hole punch, punch a hole in the dark green card stock at the top of the angel's crown. Thread a 5" piece of paper cord through the hole and twist it closed.

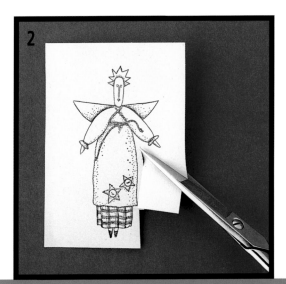

5a. Chalks:

Much like watercolor paints, chalks are easy to blend and have a light and lovely look.

1. Apply the chalk color to the image in small circles. If desired, you may apply the chalk colors using the makeup applicator. You will not have great control applying color in tiny areas, but don't let that frustrate you. Chalks look best when they are smudged and soft looking. If you wish, chalk erasers can be used to eliminate unwanted color.

2. Once you have finished applying the color, spray the image with the matte-finish sealer to permanently set the chalk.

5b. Colored Pencils:

1. It is natural to see pencil marks when you use colored pencils. Rather than fight this, use the marks to add texture to the stamped image. Crosshatching, coloring in one direction and then coloring over it in the opposite direction, produces interesting results, as does coloring an area with two coordinating colors.

2. Colored pencils should be sharpened by hand with a good pencil sharpener. You will find that sharp points and dull points produce different results. Sharp points are handy for coloring small areas. Dull points produce broader strokes of color that look softer and are easier to blend.

5c. Markers:

1. Color larger areas, using the broad tip of the marker, and smaller areas, such as the belt on the angel's gown, using the fine tip.

2. In addition to the bold color you can achieve with markers, you will enjoy the control you have in putting the color where you want it. As you color the printed image, proceed in order from the lightest color first to the darkest color last. That way, you are less likely to drag darker colors into the lighter colors.

3. Do not go over a spot with a marker too many times. The color will become very dark, and you will see the marker's brush strokes.

5d. Watercolor Paints:

Translucency and ease of blending are the two hallmarks of watercolor paints. It is easy to achieve a very soft, artistic look for a stamped image when you use watercolor paints.

1. To begin, wet the paintbrush and then make tiny circles in the color, fully loading the brush. Test it out on scrap paper to see if the color is too strong or too weak. You can always add more water or more paint to adjust the effect.

2. When painting the image, experiment with the brush strokes to see what appeals to you. Use a liner brush for getting into very small areas.

Remember, you employ watercolors to create a more unstructured, painterly result. Staying in the lines is not necessarily a goal.

3

How do I use markers to achieve a multicolored effect?

Stamped art is certain to elicit "oohs" and "aahs" when you begin adding several colors to the image. When people ask, "How did you do that?", they will be amazed when you tell them how easy it really is.

Colorful Bookmark

Here's How:

1. Ink the leaf portion of the stamp, using the side of the dark green marker.

2. Ink the berry portion of the stamp, using the side of the purple marker.

3. Give a quick puff of your breath on the image to remoisten the ink.

4. Print the image onto the bookmark.

5. Repeat as desired. You can usually get a second printing without having to reapply more ink color by puffing on the image and printing it again.

6. When you are ready to change the color of the raspberry to magenta and then to red, you will need to clean off the old color before applying the new color.

7. Using the method described for How to Thread a Gift Tag Ribbon on page 25, attach the cord of the tassel through the hole.

Troubleshooting:

- Sometimes, even though you have completely inked a bold-faced image, part of the image will not print. This leaves a spot in the middle of the printed image. You can easily fix this problem. Using the brush art marker that coordinates with the unprinted part of the image, fill in the gap with a light dotting motion directly onto the paper.

- Occasionally, a stamped bold-faced image will leave excess ink on the paper, creating little rivers of ink on the paper. You can fix this by turning the paper over, ink side down, onto a piece of scrap paper. Gently rub the back of the printed paper. All the excess ink will transfer to the scrap paper, leaving your work perfectly dry and clean.

Design Tip:

- Notice how the images are printed off the edge of the bookmark so that some of them appear only in part. This is a fun technique that draws the eye all over the bookmark, creating a more dynamic overall effect.

31

4

How do I create a watercolor look with markers?

Beautiful watercolor effects can be achieved by applying several colors of brush art markers on a single bold-faced image. The inks run together and create a palette of colors.

What You Need to Get Started:

Brush art markers:
   aqua; magenta;
   orange; pink;
   red
Card: folded
   glossy white,
   4¼" x 5½"
Dye-based ink
   pad: black
Stamps: phrase;
   star

Rainbow Star Card

Here's How:
1. Ink a small portion of the star stamp, using the side of the pink marker.

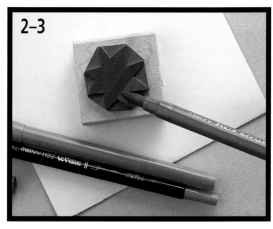

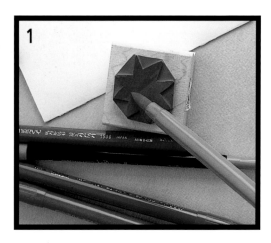

2. Beginning at the edge of where the first color left off, ink another portion of the stamp, using the orange marker.

3. Continue in this manner, using the red, magenta, and aqua markers, until the entire stamp is inked. Don't worry if the edges seem to be mixing where the marker colors meet. This adds to the watercolor effect.

4. Give a quick puff of your breath on the image to remoisten the ink.

5. Print the image onto the upper right-hand corner of the card.

6. You will probably be able to get a second printing, without having to re-apply the markers, by puffing on the image and printing again.

7. Continue coloring and stamping until the card is covered with images, using the photo opposite for placement.

8. Ink the phrase stamp, using the black ink pad. Print the image onto the lower left-hand corner of the card.

The stars exist that we might know how high our dreams can soar.

Design Tips:

- When applying many colors onto a single stamp, start with the lightest color and then continue with the midtones, saving the darkest color for last. This avoids dragging darker colors into the lighter colors, causing them to muddy.

- When printing images in a random fashion, start in the middle of the paper and work out toward the sides. Print the images at different angles to achieve a nice jumbled effect. Try to keep the spaces between the images uniform. You do not want part of your work to be densely stamped and other parts to be sparsely stamped.

technique 5

How do I heat-emboss?

Heat-embossing is a process that I still find magical after many years of rubber stamping. By sprinkling embossing powder on wet ink and then applying heat until the powder melts, you create a raised, shiny image. Heat-embossing is the type of technique that will make your friends and family exclaim "I can't believe you made this!"

Decorative Journal

Here's How:

1. Ink the stamp, using the dark blue ink pad and the following method:

- Hold the stamp with the rubber die facing you, resting it on a piece of paper. Hold the ink pad in your other hand.

- Bring the pad to the stamp and tap it lightly all over the die, making certain to ink it evenly and completely. Do not press the ink onto the die with any force as it will muddy the printed image.

2. Print the image onto the paper, taking care not to rock or twist the stamp. Give it a little muscle and then lift it straight off the paper. Don't touch the stamped image—it will smear!

3. Sprinkle the embossing powder over the stamped image.

4. Pour off the excess embossing powder either back into its container or onto a piece of scrap paper. (Fold the scrap paper in half and use it as a funnel to pour the excess powder back into the container.)

5. Preheat the heat gun for about 10 seconds and then hold it about 4" away from the stamped image. In about 15 seconds you will see the embossing powder melt, become raised and shiny, and adhere to the stamped image. Once the embossing powder is fully melted and smooth, turn off the heat gun and allow the image to cool for 30 seconds.

6. Color the printed image, using the markers and the photo below for color placement. Use the broad tip of the marker for large areas and the fine tip for smaller areas.

7. Cut out the image, using the scissors.

8. Apply adhesive to the back of the stamped image and adhere it to the front of the journal.

Troubleshooting:

- If the image is bumpy after you have heat-embossed it, you need to heat-emboss the image a little longer until all the powder is fully melted.

- If the image changes color after heat-embossing, or you smell something funny during the heat-embossing process, you are embossing the image too long. You may find that you have also scorched the paper.

- Remember, most images will heat-emboss completely after 15 seconds. There is no way to fix an over-embossed image. Start again with a fresh piece of paper.

6

How do I incorporate color into my work using embossing powders?

A stamping artist uses color in many ways to bring life to the artwork. Embossing powders are available in a myriad of hues and provide a wonderful way to add color and texture to your projects.

Heat-embossed Picture Matte

Here's How:

1. Ink a stamp, using the clear ink pad. Print one image onto the picture frame matte.

2. Pour one color of embossing powder over a portion of the stamped image. Pour the excess powder back into its container.

3. Pour the second color of embossing powder over a portion of the stamped image adjacent to the one you have just powdered. Pour off the excess

powder over the part of the image you powdered first. (Since that part of the image already has the powder affixed to it, the second color powder will not adhere to it.) Continue in this manner until the entire image is covered. You may use as many embossing powders on a single image as you like.

4. Heat-emboss the stamped image, using the heat gun.

5. Continue stamping and heat-embossing until the entire matte is covered.

Troubleshooting:

- Occasionally, you will get a stray particle of embossing powder on the piece and heat-emboss it by mistake. Once it has been heat-embossed, you cannot remove it. However, there are tricks to prevent this from happening in the future.

After pouring off the excess powder, but before heat-embossing the image, use a small dry paintbrush to brush off the stray powder or flick your fingers on the back of the stamped piece to tap it off. Also, try wiping the paper with a static-free dryer sheet before you begin stamping.

What are some simple sponging techniques I can use to create backgrounds?

Sponges are versatile tools in a stamp artist's toolbox. They can create a soft airbrushed effect or they can produce a bold, vibrant look. You can even create an entire scene with a sponge! Here I show you some different sponging techniques for producing backgrounds that help highlight photographs. Use these ideas to produce some scrapbook pages of your own.

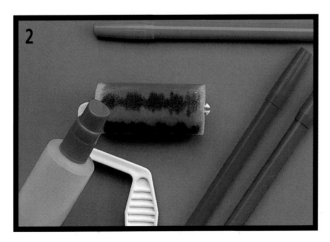

Scrapbook Page

Here's How to Create a Scrapbook Page Background:

1. Draw horizontal lines across the sponge brayer, using the light blue marker, rotating the brayer after drawing each line.

2. Lightly mist the brayer with water.

3. Roll the brayer across the scrapbook page, re-inking as necessary, until the entire page is covered.

4. Ink the brayer, using the lavender marker, and repeat the process.

5. Ink the brayer, using the dark pink marker, and repeat the process.

Here's How to Create a Scroll Frame:

1. Using the pink and yellow markers and the method described on the opposite page for Here's How to Create a Scrapbook Page Background, ink the brayer and roll it onto the card stock.

2. Ink the scroll frame stamp, using the black ink pad. Print the image over the sponging.

3. Cut out the frame, using the scissors. Apply adhesive to the back of a photograph and adhere it onto the frame. Apply adhesive to the back of the frame and adhere it onto the scrapbook page, using the photo on page 41 for placement.

Here's How to Create a Postage Stamp Frame:

1. Ink a makeup sponge, using the light pink marker. Swipe it across the card stock, leaving some white spaces between swipes.

2. Ink another sponge, using the dark pink marker. Swipe it across the card stock, filling in some of the white spaces.

3. Ink yet another sponge, using the light purple and then the dark purple markers. Swipe and fill in all the white spaces remaining on the card stock.

4. Ink the postage stamp frame stamp, using the black ink pad. Print the image onto the card stock.

5. Cut out the frame, using the scissors. Apply adhesive to the back of a photograph and adhere it onto the frame. Apply adhesive to the back of the frame and adhere it onto the scrapbook page, using the photo on page 41 for placement.

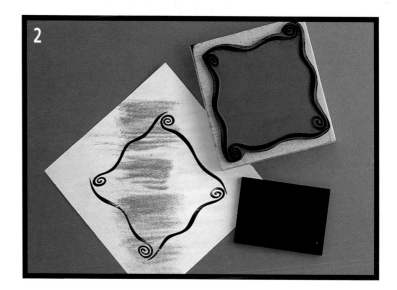

Here's How to Create a Cloud Frame:

1. Place a cloud stencil over the bottom of the card stock.

2. Ink a makeup sponge, using the peach marker. Place the inked sponge down onto the stencil. With a short swiping motion, pull the sponge away from you, off the stencil and onto the card stock. Repeat this process over the entire length of the stencil.

3. Move the stencil up and over (to the right or left, it doesn't matter). Ink a fresh piece of the sponge, using the light pink marker, and repeat the process.

4. Continue in this manner, moving the stencil and applying a new color of ink, until the entire piece of card stock is covered. It is a good idea to use no more than five colors and then repeat the colors as you move up the card.

5. Using a craft knife, cut out a cloud shape from the card stock. Outline it, using the black marker.

6. Apply adhesive to the back of a photograph and adhere it onto the cloud frame. Apply adhesive to the back of the frame and adhere it onto the scrapbook page, using the photo opposite for placement.

Here's How to Create a Deckle-edged Frame:

1. Ink a portion of the round utility sponge, using the tan marker.

2. Sponge a little ink onto scrap paper and then sponge the bottom section of a piece of card stock.

3. Ink a different portion of the sponge, using the medium blue marker. Sponge the card stock in the manner described in Step 2 to create the water section of the scene.

4. Continue in this manner, inking the sponge, using the yellow marker to sponge in the sun and the sky blue marker to sponge in the sky.

5. Ink the water stamp, using the medium blue marker; the cloud stamp, using the dark pink marker; and the sand stamps, using the peach marker. Print the images onto the scene.

6. Cut the card stock to the desired size, using scissors. Trim the edges, using the decorative-edged scissors. Using the ruler as a guide and the black marker, color the edges.

7. Apply adhesive to the back of a photograph and adhere it onto the frame. Apply adhesive to the back of the frame and adhere it onto the scrapbook page, using the photo opposite for placement.

Here's How to Finish the Page:

1. Once everything is adhered, ink the remaining small beach stamps, using the black ink pad. Print the images around and between the framed photographs.

2. Create the page caption by pressing the self-adhesive alphabet stickers as desired onto the scrapbook page.

How do I create backgrounds with a rubber brayer?

What You Need to Get Started:

Brayer: rubber, 6"-wide
Brush art markers: aqua; dark blue; royal blue; brown; cinnamon; cranberry; dark green; medium green; pea green; seafoam green; dark orange; medium orange; hot pink; red; yellow
Cards: glossy white, 5½" x 8½"
Decorative-edged scissors
Dye-based ink pad: rainbow
Embossing ink pad: clear
Glitter
Glue pen
Paper adhesive
Recipes
Ruler
Scissors
Stamps: angel; apple; leaf; muffin; palm tree
Sticker paper: glossy white

A rubber brayer is a soft rubber roller on a handle. Once ink is applied to the brayer, it allows for continuous coverage, making it an excellent tool for producing backgrounds quickly. Since this is an introductory book, I have avoided focusing on tools that have only limited application, but a brayer is so versatile, you will reach for it again and again.

Recipe Cards

Here's How:

1. Refer to the individual recipe cards on pages 43–45. Ink the brayer and roll it over the card, following the specific instructions for each card. Re-ink the brayer as necessary.

2. Type or hand-print a recipe on the paper of your choice.

3. Trim the edges of the recipe paper, using the decorative-edged scissors.

4. Apply adhesive to the back of the recipe and adhere it onto the background card.

5. Ink the coordinating stamp, using the markers and the photo on page 44 for color placement. Print the image onto sticker paper. Cut out the image, using the scissors, and press it onto the recipe card.

6. Since you will be using the cards in the kitchen, you may want to laminate them to keep them clean.

Trouble Shooting:

• A brayer should be stored with the metal bar down so that the wheel doesn't rest against anything, which might cause an unwanted impression in the rubber.

Here's How to Make a Recipe Book:

A handmade recipe book makes a great gift for the bride-to-be, a new neighbor, or a thoughtful friend. There are several ways to turn your stamped recipe cards into a book:

• Purchase a photo album with pocket pages that are the right size to hold the cards.

• Punch a hole in the top left hand corner of the card and insert either a locking ring (available at any hardware store) or a pretty ribbon.

• Look for a sturdy folder at the stationery store to hold the cards.

1a. Baked Apple Card:

1. Ink the apple stamp, using the red marker. Hold the inked stamp on the table with the die side up and roll the brayer across the stamp several times, moving the brayer each time, so that the image appears on different parts of the brayer.

2. Roll the brayer across the length of the card several times until the brayer is too dry to print. Re-ink the stamp and repeat the process.

3. Ink the apple stamp, using the medium green marker. Repeat the brayering process.

4. Ink the apple stamp, using the yellow marker. Repeat the brayering process.

5. Using a ruler as your guide and the medium green marker, draw a border around the card.

See photo on page 44.

1a. Design Tips:
• Using stamps and a brayer together in this manner produces a soft watercolor look. To give your background a focal point, try stamping some apples directly onto the card. They will seem to pop out of the brayered background.

• Remember that when you roll a brayer over an inked stamp and then roll it onto paper, the image reverses. A flower that may lean to the left on the stamp is going to lean to the right once brayered. This can be a lovely effect when brayered images are combined with stamped images.

1b. Blueberry Muffin Card:

1. Hold the brayer so that the roller spins freely.

2. Draw a tight, squiggly line along one edge of the brayer, using the brown marker. Turn the brayer so that you can continue to draw the line until it becomes an unbroken circle.

3. Draw three more lines evenly spaced along the brayer, using the brown marker.

4. Between the brown lines, continue drawing lines in the same manner, using the dark blue, royal blue, and cranberry markers.

5. Roll the brayer along the length of the card. Once you have covered the card horizontally, turn the card so you can repeat the process vertically.

See photo on page 44.

1b. Design Tip:
• Try inking the brayer with straight lines, a herringbone pattern, or curvy lines. You may want to make the background with just horizontal or vertical lines. Experiment and design your own backgrounds.

Best Blueberry Muffins

1. Preheat oven to 350. butter muffin tins
2. Cream 6 T. butter and 3/4 C. sugar
3. Beat in 2 eggs, one at a time
4. In a separate bowl, whisk 2 C. flour 2 t. baking powder, and 1/2 t. salt
5. Add dry ingredients to the wet ingredients and beat well.
6. Stir in 1/2 C. milk and 2 t. vanilla until smooth.
7. Stir in 2 C. berries.
8. Fill muffin cups half way.
9. Sprinkle muffins tops with 1 T. sugar mixed with 1 t. cinnamon
10. Bake for 30 minutes

Hearty Autumn Soup

...ace 1 chopped onion, 2 peeled and diced sweet potatoes and 4
C. of vegetable... ...t in a saucepan and boil.
Reduce heat, co... ...er for 25 minutes.
Cool slightly an... ...until smooth.
Return to sau... ...and half.
Season with ... ...ice to taste. Serve
warm.

Best Baked Apples Ever

Core a tart, firm apple. Place it in a saucepan.
Pour 2 cups of apple cider into the pan.
Place 1 vanilla bean, 1 T. vanilla sugar and
1 T. of butter into the cavity of the apple.
Cover and cook on a medium flame for 30 minutes.
Serve warm with whipped cream or sour cream.

1c. Hearty Autumn Soup Card:

1. Ink the leaf stamp, using the clear ink pad. Print the image all over the card. Do not heat-emboss the leaf images.

2. Ink the brayer, using a rainbow pad with an autumn hue. Roll it over the leaves. The embossing ink resists the brayered ink, causing the leaves to appear with a ghostly shadow.

1c. Design Tip:

• Ink the stamp, using the clear ink pad. Heat-emboss the stamped leaf images with clear embossing powder for a more pronounced leaf image. Proceed with brayering technique.

1d. Heavenly Brickle Bar Card:

1. Holding the brayer with the metal bar resting on the table, draw little clouds all over the brayer, using the aqua and seafoam green markers.

2. Roll the brayer back and forth over the card until it is completely filled.

3. Outline several clouds, using the glue pen. Sprinkle glitter over the glue. Pour the excess glitter back into the container.

1d. Design Tip:

• Instead of clouds, draw squiggles, dots, dashes, or any other design you desire onto the brayer. Roll the brayer over the card as desired to create an instant patterned background.

1e. Tropical Fruit Salsa Card:

1. Roll the brayer across the rainbow ink pad, making certain you are rolling with the stripes of the pad. (Rolling against them will cause the inks to mix and become muddy.) Once you get to the end of the pad, pick up the brayer and begin again, repeating the process at least four more times until the brayer is fully covered.

2. Roll the brayer back and forth across the length of the card, pressing hard, until the card is completely covered.

1e. Design Tips:

• Try printing the card on the diagonal or create a brayered plaid by rolling the brayer both horizontally and vertically.

• If the brayer does not cover the entire width of the card, turn the paper around, re-ink the brayer, and roll the brayer to cover the remaining part of the card.

How do I use stamps to create a background?

What You Need to Get Started:

Bone folder
Corner rounder
  punch
Decorative paper:
  navy blue (for
  journal title);
  yellow (for
  journal cover)
Dye-based ink
  pads: black;
  navy blue;
  cranberry;
  green; plum
Foam tape
Heavy cardboard:
  4½" x 5½" (2)
Heavy paper:
  black, 30" x 4¼"
Paper adhesive
Ruler
Scissors
Stamps: faux
  passport; faux
  postage;
  large photo
  frame; "Bon
  voyage!"
  phrase

An image doesn't always have to have a starring role in a piece of stamped art. By overlapping images, you can create a dynamic background that comes together quickly. As you are choosing images to overlap, don't overlook word stamps—they make very strong statements! Once you have created this background, layer one or two important images on top and your project is complete.

Travel Photo Journal

Here's How:
1. To make the front and back journal covers, cut the yellow paper to 1" larger than the cardboard on all sides and center one piece of cardboard on each piece of the yellow paper. Trim off the corners of each piece of the paper. Apply adhesive to each edge of the paper. Fold down the overlapping edges of the paper and adhere them to the cardboard.

2. Using a bone folder and ruler, fold the long black paper accordion-style into six equal sections of 5" x 4¼", making certain to begin and end with valley folds.

3. Apply glue to the back side of one end (the first page) of the folded paper and adhere it to the back of the front cover. Adhere the remaining end to the back of the back cover. The journal is now constructed.

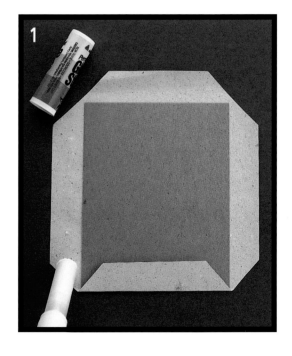

4. Ink the faux-postage and faux-passport stamps, using the ink colors of your choice. Randomly print the images onto the cover, making certain to overlap the images.

5. Ink the phrase stamp, using the black

ink pad. Print the image onto a separate piece of the yellow paper for the journal's title. Trim the corners, using a corner rounder punch.

6. Apply glue to the back of the stamped title and adhere it onto the navy blue paper. Trim those corners as well.

7. Attach the title to the front cover with several pieces of foam tape.

8. To create photo mattes, ink the photo frame stamp, using the black ink pad. Print the image six times onto the yellow paper. Cut out the images, using the scissors.

9. Apply adhesive to the back of the photo mattes and adhere them onto each journal page.

10. Apply adhesive to the back of the photographs from a favorite trip and adhere them onto the photo mattes.

Here's How to Ensure a Long Life for Your Paper Creations:

Whenever you are creating something that you want to last a lifetime and particularly when you are working with photographs, it is imperative that you select the right materials and storage options to ensure these fragile papers a long life.

"Archival quality," "pH balanced," and "acid free" are terms that describe the inks, papers, and adhesives you should use in these special projects. These terms will help you identify products that contain little or no acid, an enemy of paper. Keep in mind, however, that no product can guarantee that the papers will last forever. You can take an extra precautionary step by using acid-free, buffered paper (a paper that helps absorb and neutralize acid).

Another enemy of paper and photographs is sunlight. So whenever possible, keep your paper keepsakes out of direct sunlight. Of course, the most dangerous element paper can come into contact with is any moisture, so take care to keep all paper creations dry. By taking these few precautionary steps, you will help your paper art live a long life.

How do I create borders with paper layering?

Paper layering is an easy technique that adds a professional polish to the simplest piece of stamped art. Just as matting and a picture frame finish off a piece of artwork you might hang on a wall, paper layering completes the art you are creating by adding a paper border. I have used a single image for a greeting card and show it to you without any paper layering. I also offer five different approaches for the same image, incorporating a variety of paper layering techniques, with each technique varying the look of my card.

Birdhouse Greeting Card

Here's How to Make a Basic Card:
1. Ink the birdhouse stamp, using the brown ink pad. Print the image onto an off-white folded card.

2. Using the watercolor paint set, paint the image, taking care to clean the paintbrush when changing to a new color.

   This example shows the stamped image on an off-white card without any paper layering. Compared to the other examples, it is rather plain.

Here's How to Add Layers:

1. Ink the birdhouse stamp, using the brown ink pad. Print the image onto the off-white card stock.

2. Using the watercolor paint set, paint the image, taking care to clean the paintbrush when changing to a new color.

3. Trim the off-white card stock to a rectangle about ½" larger than the image, using the decorative-edged scissors.

4. Apply adhesive to the back of the off-white card stock and adhere it onto a piece of the dark plum card stock.

5. Trim the dark plum card stock, using the decorative-edged scissors, so that it is about ⅛" larger than the off-white card stock.

6. Apply adhesive to the back of the dark plum card stock and adhere these two layers off center onto the front of a lavender folded card.

Here's How to Silhouette:

1. Ink the birdhouse stamp, using the brown ink pad. Print the image onto the off-white card stock.

2. Using the watercolor paint set, paint the image, taking care to clean the paintbrush when changing to a new color.

3. Cut out the image, using the decorative-edged scissors, leaving about ¼" of the off-white card stock all around the edge.

4. Apply adhesive to the back of the off-white card stock and adhere it onto a piece of the green polka-dot card stock.

5. Trim the green polka-dot card stock, using the decorative-edged scissors, so that it is about ½" smaller on each side than the folded card.

6. Apply adhesive to the back of the green polka-dot card stock and adhere these two layers onto the front of a gold folded card.

Here's How to Add Texture:

1. Ink the birdhouse stamp, using the brown ink pad. Print the image onto the off-white card stock.

2. Using the watercolor paint set, paint the image, taking care to clean the paintbrush when changing to a new color.

3. Trim the off-white card stock to a rectangle about ½" larger than the image, using the decorative-edged scissors.

4. Using the scissors, cut a piece of brown corrugated card stock, slightly smaller than the stamped and trimmed off-white card stock. Apply adhesive to the back of each. Place each piece of card stock on opposing diagonals and adhere them onto a dark green folded card.

5. Using a hole punch, punch half of a hole along the folded edge of the card about one-third and two-thirds of the way down. Thread raffia through the holes. Tie it into a bow.

Here's How to Use Multiple Images:

1. Ink the birdhouse stamp, using the brown ink pad. Print the image onto the off-white card stock.

2. Using the watercolor paint set, paint the image, taking care to clean the paintbrush when changing to a new color.

3. Trim the off-white card stock to a rectangle about ½" larger than the image, using the decorative-edged scissors.

4. Ink the daisy cluster stamp, using the brown ink pad. Print the image all around the edge of an off-white folded card. Paint the images, using the watercolor paint set.

5. Apply adhesive to the back of the stamped and trimmed off-white card stock and adhere it to a piece of the sage green card stock. Trim it all around, using the scissors, so it is ½" larger than the off-white card stock. Apply adhesive to the back of the sage green card stock and adhere these two layers onto the stamped folded card.

Here's How to Embellish:

1. Ink the birdhouse stamp, using the brown ink pad. Print the image onto the off-white card stock.

2. Using the watercolor paint set, paint the image, taking care to clean the paintbrush when changing to a new color.

3. Trim the off-white card stock to a rectangle about ½" larger than the image, using the decorative-edged scissors.

4. Apply adhesive to the back of the stamped and trimmed off-white card stock and adhere it onto a piece of gold card stock. Using the scissors, trim the gold card stock so it is about ⅛" larger than the off-white card stock. Apply adhesive to the back of the gold card stock and adhere these two layers onto an olive green folded card.

5. Using a hole punch, punch an even number of holes, evenly spaced, along all edges of the olive green card. Starting at the upper left-hand corner, thread several pieces of raffia in and out through the holes. Tie a bow at the corner where the ends meet.

Here's How to Score and Fold a Card:

You can easily make greeting cards by hand in the color and size of your choosing by using a bone folder and a piece of card stock.

Cards that are not properly folded have a jagged, folded edge and may look as though the paper has been slightly frayed and torn. The trick to making a professional-looking card is all in the scoring and folding.

1. Use a piece of card stock that, once folded in half, will be a bit larger than the card you want to make. Mark off the center very lightly, using a pencil.

2. Hold a ruler down on the center of the card, following the marks you have just made.

3. Using a bone folder, make a line on the paper against the edge of the ruler. You have just broken the outside fibers of the papers enough so that it will fold easily.

4. The score line you have just made will be the outside fold, or mountain fold, of the card. Fold the card stock along the score line and use the bone folder to smooth down the fold.

5. Trim the card down to the size you desire, using a paper cutter.

How do I stamp borders?

Stamping borders is a simple and effective way to decorate projects. The tools you need to accomplish the precise placement of the image into a border are a stamp positioner and a clear plastic square. They are often sold together as a set. A stamp positioner is a thick acrylic corner that creates a 90° angle. In addition to creating borders, a stamp positioner is also useful if you want to combine images, such as placing a little girl exactly on a swing or positioning a ball precisely into a clown's hand.

Bordered Picture Frame Card

Here's How:
1. Place the stamp positioner so that the corner is near your left hand and one side of the positioner is horizontal and the other side vertical.

2. Slide the plastic square so that it fits snugly into the 90° angle created by the stamp positioner.

3. Ink the stamp and fit it snugly into the 90° angle of the stamp positioner. Print the image onto the plastic square. (You will wash it off the square when you are finished with your project.)

4. Beginning at the top of the heart-shaped window of the picture frame card, place the plastic square so that the image appears exactly where you want it.

5. Fit the stamp positioner snugly around the corner of the stamped plastic square. Remove the plastic square.

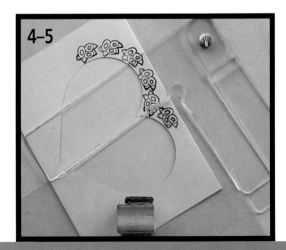

6. Ink the stamp and place it snugly into the 90° corner of the stamp positioner. Print the image.

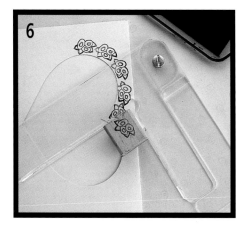

7. Lift off the stamp positioner. The image should be exactly where you wanted it!

8. Continue in this manner, placing the plastic square and the stamp positioner around the window of the frame card. Print the images until the border is complete.

9. Print an additional image in each lower corner of the card.

10. Color the images, using the colored pencils.

Troubleshooting— Here's How to Fix Smudges and Unwanted Lines:

You are nearing the completion of your card and it looks terrific. While printing one of the last images, your hand jumps and you print some unwanted lines. Don't despair. There are a few ways you can correct this:

- A white correction pen can cover small lines and smudges effectively.

- Try sponging on a background color and thereby soften the effect of the unwanted lines.

- Work the lines into a patterned background that you put in by hand.

- Incorporate the unwanted lines into the images, using a coordinating pen.

- Cut the image away from the offending background and use it as a motif.

12

What are some simple borders that I can create?

What You Need to Get Started:

Brush art markers: light blue; dark green; grass green; light green; orange; pink; purple; red; violet; yellow
Card stock: glossy white, 2¾" x 4"; scraps
Craft adhesive
Craft knife
Cutting mat
Dual-tipped markers: black; purple
Embossing markers: clear; green; red
Embossing powder: clear
Foamcore board
Glue pen
Heat gun
Lollipop sticks
Makeup sponge: wedge-shaped
Paper adhesive
Pinking shears
Ruler
Spray acrylic sealer: matte finish
Stamps: daisy; hydrangea; rose; tulip
Ultra-fine glitter: yellow

Nothing gives a more tailored look to a project than a border. Somehow a border focuses your work and completes it at the same time. Creating borders can be as simple or as complex as you wish it to be. Below I show you some fast and easy border ideas. Once you are comfortable with these, try them in variations or combinations and you will be delighted with the beautiful effects you can produce!

Plant Markers

Here's How:
1. Ink the flower stamp, using the brush art markers. Print the image onto the white card stock.

2. Refer to the individual flowers on pages 54–55. Add the border, following the specific instructions for each plant marker.

3. Write the name of the flower, using the black dual-tipped marker.

4. Spray the plant marker with a coat of matte-finish sealer. Allow it to dry.

5. Place the foam core board on a cutting mat and cut a piece slightly smaller than the plant marker, using the craft knife with a fresh blade.

6. Push one end of the lollipop stick into the center of the piece of foam-core board so that it makes a 1" in-dentation. Remove the stick, dip one end into the craft adhesive and then re-insert that end into the foamcore board. Allow it to dry for several hours.

7. Apply paper adhesive to the back of each plant marker and adhere them onto the foamcore boards.

2a. Daisy:
1. Position the ruler along the edge of the card and draw a border, using the yellow brush art marker. Go over the lines you have just drawn, using a glue pen. Sprinkle the yellow glitter over the card. Pour the excess glitter back into the container. Allow the card to dry for several minutes.

2b. Hydrangea:
1. Position the ruler ¼" from the border. Using the fine tip of the purple dual-tipped marker, draw a border around the edge of the card, leaving a little space around any leaves or stems that are stamped off the edge of the card.

2c. Rose:

1. Position the ruler along the edge of the card and draw a border, using the red embossing marker. Heat-emboss it with clear embossing powder, using the heat gun. Set the ruler in slightly in from the red border and draw in a green border, using the green embossing marker. Heat-emboss it with clear embossing powder, using the heat gun.

2d. Tulip:

1. Trim one edge of a piece of scrap paper, using pinking shears. Generously ink about 1" of one side of a makeup sponge, using the pink marker. Using the scrap paper as a stencil, swipe the sponge over the pinked edge of the paper, creating the zigzag image on the card.

Variations:

1. Ink the makeup sponge, using the embossing ink. Using a pinked edge of scrap paper as a stencil, swipe the sponge over it, creating a zigzag border on the card. Heat-emboss the zigzag border.

2. Cut scrap paper, using any decorative-edged scissors. Use the cut edge as a stencil.

3. Draw a border of dots and dashes with the black dual-tipped marker for a "stitched" look.

4. Make a border, using the clear embossing marker. Sprinkle several colors of embossing powder onto the ink and heat-emboss.

5. Make a border with a layer of double-sided tape. Sprinkle tiny beads, flecks of mica, or any one of the many available textured add-ons onto the tape.

13

How do I enhance my stamped art with shadows and shading?

What You Need to Get Started:

Buttons: small
Card stock: white
Colored pencils:
  light blue;
  brown; gray;
  pink; dark purple;
  dark yellow
Craft adhesive
Cup of water
Decorative-edged
  scissors: scallop
Decorative papers:
  blue; pink
Fine-line pen:
  brown
Hole punch: ¼"
Paintbrush: small
Paper adhesive
Paper gift bags:
  light blue; pink
Permanent ink
  pad: brown
Ribbon: light blue
Ruler
Scissors
Stamps: baby and
  blanket; baby
  and parachute;
  baby shoes (small
  and large);
  carriage; diaper
  pin; heart with
  wings; "Heaven
  sent from up
  above;" "It's a
  Boy;" star; word
  banner; "Yippee"
Watercolor pencils:
  light blue; light
  brown

To really give your stamped art an artist's finish, there is no technique better than adding shadows or shading. The images will look grounded instead of floating on the page. Don't be intimidated—you do not need an art degree to be able to add just the right touch of visual dimension! Many stamps provide the shading lines within the image and others can be shaded simply with a gray colored pencil.

Gift Bags for New Babies

Here's How to Make the Blue Bag:

1. Using scissors, cut the card stock 1½" smaller than the size of the gift bag (measuring from the handles).

2. Ink the stamps, using the brown ink pad. Print the images onto the white card stock, using the photo opposite for placement.

3. Using the brown pen and a ruler to guide you, draw "stitch" marks around the images. Make certain that all of the horizontal lines and vertical lines are parallel to each other.

4. Color the images, using the colored pencils.

5. Using the gray colored pencil, add shadows to the stamped images.

Generally, if the imagined light source is in the upper left-hand corner, you should add the shadow next to the bottom and lower right side of the image.

6. Apply paper adhesive to the back of the stamped and colored card stock and adhere it

56

onto a piece of pink decorative paper. Trim the paper, using the decorative-edged scissors, so it is slightly larger than the card stock. Apply paper adhesive to the back of the pink paper and adhere it onto the bag.

7. Apply craft adhesive to the backs of the buttons and adhere them onto the bag.

Design Tips:

- Feel free to experiment with shadows since colored pencils can be erased easily with a white artist's eraser.

- When you want a soft effect for the outline stamps, try using a brown ink pad. It provides a subtle but effective difference. Save the black ink pad for images that require a stronger contrast.

Here's How to Make the Pink Bag:

1. Ink the shoes and phrase stamps, using the brown ink pad. Print the images onto separate pieces of card stock.

2. Color the shaded areas of the printed shoe image, using the light blue watercolor pencil. Color the soles of the shoes, using the light brown watercolor pencil.

3. Wet a small paintbrush and sweep it over the watercolor pencil lines so that they soften and begin to flow together. Leave the areas of the shoes with more shading a darker

blue, while pulling some of the color into the unshaded part of the shoe. Make certain that the parts of the shoe that would be highlighted are left white.

4. Trim around each image, using the decorative-edged scissors. Apply paper adhesive to the back of each and adhere them onto layered pink and blue decorative papers that have also been trimmed so each is slightly larger than the other.

5. Using the hole punch, punch

two holes in the center of the card stock with the shoe image about ½" apart from each other. Thread a 3" piece of ribbon through the holes from the front to the back. Cross the ribbon ends and feed them back through the holes from the back to the front.

6. Apply paper adhesive to the back of each piece of light blue decorative paper and adhere each onto the front of the bag, using the photo below for placement.

How do I create a scene with rubber stamps?

You can create scenes by combining stamped images. The scenes can range from a simple juxtaposition of several images to an elaborate, realistic work of art. A few techniques will help you make the stamps work towards reproducing the scene you envision. You will learn how to make and use masks, use multiple prints from a single inking, and create the illusion of depth with intensity of color.

Video Tape Cover

Here's How:

1. Ink the bear, campfire, and television stamps, using the black ink pad. Print the images onto the card stock. These are foreground images.

2. Print each of those images onto self-adhesive notes (a separate note for each image), making certain that a portion of the image is printed over the part of the note backed with adhesive. Cut out each image. You have just created masks for these images.

3. Place each mask over the corresponding image. (The adhesive part of the mask will hold it in place.) Ink the tree stamp, using the grass green, blue green, and light green markers. Print the image next to and over the masked bear. Don't worry—when you remove the mask, the images will look like they are in the background, behind the masked image. Without re-inking the stamp,

print two more sets of trees. They will appear faded and further away than the first set of trees.

4. Remove the bear's mask to reveal a forest with depth.

5. Replace the bear's mask. Ink the rocks and hot dog stamps, using the black ink pad. Print these images onto the card stock.

6. Make a mask for the rocks and adhere them to the corresponding images. Ink the grass stamp, using the light green marker. Randomly print the image. Re-ink the grass stamp, using the grass green marker. Print the image towards the bottom of the card. Because it is darker, this section of the grass will appear closer to the viewer. Ink the grass stamp, using the blue green marker. Print the image a few times to add more dimension to the grass.

7. Ink the sponge, using the brown ink pad. Sponge the grass and campfire area to make the ground look more realistic. Remove all masks.

8. Ink a clean section of the sponge, using the sage green ink pad. Sponge in the sky, making certain to sponge over the trees and right up to the grass so that there is no area of the scene left uncolored. You have created a natural-looking horizon line.

9. Color the images, using colored pencils, markers, and the photo on page 61 for placement.

10. Place the television mask on the cutting mat and cut out the screen portion, using the craft knife. Discard the screen. You have just created what is called a "mortise" mask. It will allow you to stamp inside the television screen without overlapping onto the television cabinet.

11. Place the mortise mask over the television. Ink the water-skier stamp, using the black ink pad, and the water stamp, using the aqua ink pad. Print these images within the television screen. Ink the small cloud stamp, using the sage green ink pad. Print the image within the television. Color the sky, using a light blue colored pencil, and the water, using a medium blue colored pencil. Remove the mask.

12. For the video's title, ink the alphabet stamps, using the black ink pad. Print the images onto the cover.

Design Tips:

- Developing a scene takes a bit of fore-thought and planning. Decide on two or three images which will be the central focus of the scene. These elements will probably be placed in the foreground. Then, choose the images you want to use in producing the background.

- If it is an outdoor scene, remember that you will need to create the ground and the sky, which must meet at the horizon line. Interior scenes also have a horizon line, where the walls and floor meet. This can be drawn or stamped.

- Most scenes you design will require a proper sense of perspective. Smaller and lighter images appear farther away, while larger and darker images appear closer. Choose stamps that support the sense of per-spective you are trying to create. Try to balance size, color intensity, and layout so that the primary elements draw the viewer's focus, and the background elements set the stage.

Layout:

A great way to help you arrange the layout for the scene is to first print each image on scrap paper and cut them out. Position them on a test sheet of card stock until you are pleased with the scene. Tape the pieces down and use this test sheet as a guide for your stamped art. Experiment with coloring ideas on this sheet as well.

Remember, when making a stamped scene always start with the foreground and work backwards, layering the background images behind the foreground images.

Masks:

When cutting masks, cut through several layers of self-adhesive notes at one time, creating duplicate masks. When one becomes dirty or torn, you have another one ready to go. Save the clean masks on a clean sheet of card stock.

When cutting masks, cut them out on the inside of the image's outline. They will be slightly smaller than the original. When you use these masks, you will be able to stamp back-grounds that come right to the edge of the foreground image without an undesirable halo effect as shown right.

Masks can be useful if you want only part of an image to print. Cover the part of the paper you don't want printed with the mask. Ink the stamp, and print the image, printing the un-wanted part of the image onto the mask. Lift the mask and you have produced a partial image. This technique can work particularly well when you are printing borders and don't want the corners to be printed twice (once from the vertical printing and again from the horizontal printing). Mask the corner after it has been printed once and print the second corner over the mask. Voila! A perfect border.

Multiple Prints from a Single Inking:

This can be an effective technique for showing motion. Ink and print the main image first, then without re-inking the stamp, print two or more impressions behind it and slightly overlapping as shown right. The blurred impression produces the illusion of movement.

How can I use one stamp effectively to design an entire project?

What You Need to Get Started:

Beads: assorted
Bone folder
Card stock: sage green; rust; flecked tan, 5½" x 8½"
Dye-based ink pad: black
Embossing ink pad: clear
Embossing powders: jasper; verdigris
Folded note cards, 4¼" x 3½": sage green; rust
Heat gun
Paper adhesive
Plastic: clear square
Raffia: rust
Ruler
Scissors
Stamp: bear claw
Stamp positioner
Stationery paper: flecked tan with coordinating envelope

Even after you have amassed your stamp collection, you will find that it can be challenging and fun to design an entire project using just one stamp. You will also be pleasantly surprised at the different looks you can achieve with a single image by varying layout, color, and texture.

Bear Claw Stationery Set

Here's How to Make the Greeting Card:

1. Ink the stamp, using the black ink pad. Print the image onto the plastic square, using the stamp positioner.

2. Using the bone folder and ruler, score and fold the flecked tan card stock in half to create a card.

3. Ink the stamp, using the clear embossing ink pad. Print the image along the front of the card, using the stamp positioner and the plastic square. Heat-emboss the images, using the jasper embossing powder for the bottom and top rows and the verdigris embossing powder for the middle row.

4. Using the scissors, trim the triangular shapes from the bottom of the card.

5. Cut a piece of the sage green card stock to fit the inside of the card. Apply adhesive to the back of the card stock and adhere it to the inside of the card. Cut a piece of the rust card stock to fit over the back of the card with a small overhang, forming a border on the bottom. Apply adhesive to the back of the card stock and adhere it onto the back of the card.

Here's How to Make the Small Folded Card:

1. Ink the stamp, using the embossing ink pad. Print the image in the upper left-hand corner of the folded note card.

2. Heat-emboss the image, using the verdigris embossing powder on the rust card and the jasper embossing powder on the sage green card.

Here's How to Make the Stationery:

1. Ink the stamp, using the black ink pad. Print the image onto the plastic square, using the stamp positioner.

2. Ink the stamp, using the embossing ink pad. Print the image along the top and bottom of the stationery paper and on the envelope flap, using the photo opposite for placement. Heat-emboss the images, using the jasper and verdigris embossing powders and the heat gun.

3. Tie the decorated sheets of stationery together with raffia. Tie coordinating beads to the ends of the raffia.

Design Tips:

- As an exercise in creativity, try designing a few other cards, each with a unique look but composed of the same materials. Think about what appeals to you in each card. This will help you develop your own individual style.

- Don't overlook the impact of forming a circle with the stamped image as shown right. Suddenly the single image takes on a whole new dimension.

- As you experiment with the layout of your cards, notice how the negative space (the blank space between the stamped images) becomes as much a part of the design as the image itself. When you are using only one image, the area you don't stamp is as important as the one you do!

How do I incorporate collage elements with stamping?

What You Need to Get Started:

Adhesive foam dots
Angel hair: gold
Card stock: off-white, 5" x 7"
Charms: brass sun; tiny brass star
Craft adhesive
Cup of water
Embossing powder: clear
Handmade papers: different patterns of black and gold (3)
Heat gun
Paintbrush: small
Paper adhesive
Photo album: black, spiral bound
Pigment ink pad: copper
Pigment powder: gold
Scissors
Shaped confetti: large gold star
Stamps: checkerboard star; dotted star; sun

Collage is a French word that literally means "pasting." Collage is a process in which papers and found objects are pasted together to form a pleasing whole. By providing central or background images, stamping can enhance the beauty of a collage.

Celestial Photo Album

Here's How:

1. Tear irregular-shaped pieces from each of the handmade papers, using the following method:

- Place the paper on a clean surface. Load a small paintbrush with water and brush on the line where you want the tear to be.

- Hold the paper in place with a hand on one side of the water line and gently pull the opposite side with the other hand. The paper should tear easily and leave an interesting edge with the fibers fanned out. Allow the paper to dry before you use it in the project.

2. Ink the sun, checkerboard star, and dotted star stamps, using the copper ink pad. Print the images onto the off-white card stock (print the checkerboard star twice). Heat-emboss the images, using the embossing powder and a heat gun. Allow them to cool.

3. Using the scissors, cut out the stars, leaving as little card stock border as possible.

4. Gently tear out the sun, leaving about a ¼" card stock border. To achieve a deckle-edged effect around the sun, hold the paper in your left hand with the image facing you and carefully tear it toward you with your right hand.

5. Dip your pinkie finger into the gold pigment powder and gently rub it over all of the stamped images.

6. Place the three pieces of handmade paper over the photo album cover so that they overlap and form a pleasing, balanced composition. Apply adhesive to the back of each and adhere them in place.

7. Apply adhesive to the center of the back of the sun image and adhere the angel hair.

8. Apply adhesive foam dots to the back of the sun image, one of the checkerboard stars, and the confetti star. Attach them to the album, using the photo below for placement.

9. Apply craft adhesive to the remaining checkerboard star and the dotted star and adhere them onto the album. Apply craft adhesive to the two brass charms and adhere them in place.

10. Using the scissors, trim off any handmade paper that may be overlapping the sides of the album.

17

How do I create die-cuts with rubber stamps?

Make your stamped art stand up and really grab attention. By cutting out part of an image and folding the rest of it back, you create a die-cut. You also create quite a sensation at a spooky Halloween party!

Halloween Party Ideas

Here's How to Make Invitations:

1. Ink the gravestone and "Trick or Treat" phrase stamps, using the black ink pad. Print the images onto the white card stock. Heat-emboss the images, using the embossing powder and the heat gun.

2. Make a mask for the gravestone. Ink, print, and heat-emboss the ghost image so it appears to be behind the gravestone.

3. Ink, print, and heat-emboss the spider image next to the gravestone. Draw the spider thread, using the black marker.

4. Color all images, using the markers and the photo opposite for placement.

5. Score the center back side of the card stock (up to the gravestone but not across it), using the bone folder and the ruler. Place the ghost image on the cutting mat and cut around the top of the image to the score line, using the craft knife. Fold along the score line so the ghost's head pops up. Blacken the exposed edges of the ghost's head, using the black marker.

6. Cut off the excess card stock, using the scissors, so that the folded card now measures 3" x 5".

7. Score and fold the gold card stock in half and cut it to 3¼" x 5¼", using the scissors. Apply adhesive to the front of the gold card stock and adhere it to the underside of the stamped card.

8. Score and fold the purple card stock in half and cut it to 3½" x 5½", using the scissors. Apply adhesive to the front of the purple card stock and adhere it to the underside of the gold card stock.

9. Ink, print, and heat-emboss the "You're Invited" phrase under the gravestone.

10. Ink, print, and heat-emboss four candy corn images onto remaining white card stock. Color each candy corn, using markers and the photo opposite for placement. Using the scissors, cut out the images. Adhere them to the card, using the foam tape.

11. Sponge in the background, using the green and brown markers.

Here's How to Make Placecards:

1. Ink, print, and heat-emboss the witch face image onto the white card stock.

Color the image, using the photo for placement.

2. Score the center back side of the card stock (up to the witch face but not across it), using the bone folder and the ruler. Place the witch face image on the cutting mat. Cut around the hat to the score line, using the craft knife. Fold the card stock so the witch's hat pops up. Blacken the exposed edges of the hat, using the black marker.

3. Cut the folded card to 1¾" x 3½", using the scissors.

4. Sponge in the background, using the yellow and orange markers.

5. Score and fold the purple card stock in half and cut it to 2" x 3¾", using the scissors. Apply adhesive to the front of the purple card stock and adhere it to the underside of the stamped card.

6. Write the guest's name on the stamped card, using the black marker.

Here's How to Make Napkin Rings:

1. Ink, print, and heat-emboss the pumpkin image onto the white card stock. Color the images, using markers and the photo for placement.

2. Draw a 1" x 4" tab on each side of the pumpkin head. These tabs will form the ring around the napkin.

3. Cut out the pumpkin with the tabs, using the scissors. Blacken the exposed edges of the pumpkin, using the black marker.

4. Place the pumpkin on the cutting mat and cut a small portion of the pumpkin's sides away from the tab, using the craft knife, making certain that the top and bottom of the tabs are still attached.

5. Sponge in the background, using the purple marker.

6. Apply adhesive to the tabs and adhere them together. Insert a napkin through the ring.

Here's How to Make a Table Decoration:

1. Ink, print, and heat-emboss five pumpkin images in a row, 1" apart, onto the white card

stock. Color the images, using the markers and the photo for placement.

2. Place the pumpkins on the cutting mat and cut out the left-hand side of each pumpkin, using the craft knife. Blacken the exposed edges, using the black marker. Score the right-hand side.

3. Fold the images accordion style.

4. Using the scissors, trim off the top and bottom edges of the paper, slightly above and below the pumpkins.

5. Sponge in the background, using the purple marker.

How can I add dimension to my stamped art?

What You Need to Get Started:

Beads: tiny gold
Card stock: gold; ivory
Chalk: light blue
Corrugated cardboard: dark green
Craft adhesive: white
Dual-tipped marker: black
Embossing markers: gold; dark green; light green; orange; yellow
Embossing powder: clear
Foam tape
Frame of choice
Heat gun
Makeup applicator: sponge-tipped
Paper adhesive
Pigment ink pad: black
Pinking shears
Scissors
Spoon
Stamps: phrase; sunflower

Dimension is a wonderful element to incorporate into your stamped projects. There are many exciting tools and materials available that will help you add that extra bit of texture you are looking for. Keep your eyes open for yarns and wire, puff paint and flocking, acetate and mica tiles, and all sorts of textural elements that can be used to make your artwork jump off the paper.

Framed Sunflowers

Here's How:
1. Ink the sunflower stamp, using the black ink pad. Print the image onto ivory card stock. Heat-emboss the image, using the embossing powder and the heat gun. Allow the image to cool. Repeat for a second image.

2. Using the make-up applicator, rub the chalk lightly into the background areas of each image, producing a hint of color.

3. Color one image completely, using the embossing markers and the photo opposite for placement. Heat-emboss the image using the embossing powder and heat gun.

4. Color and heat-emboss the second image. Allow it to cool. Then, cut out only the flowers, using the scissors.

5. With the colored side laying in the palm of your hand, rub the bowl of a spoon into the back of the cut-out flowers, causing the flower centers to push out. Turn the flowers over and curl the petals slightly inward towards the center.

6. Blacken the edges of the cut-out flowers, using the black marker.

7. Apply three layers of the foam tape onto the back of the cut-out flowers, making certain the tape does not show from the front. Attach the cut-out flowers on top of the first image.

8. Using the scissors, cut out the leaf from the second image. Blacken the edges of the leaf, using the black

marker. Apply paper adhesive to the back of the leaf base and adhere it onto the uncut image. Curl the end of the leaf out.

9. Dilute the craft adhesive and spread a bit onto the center of the dimensional flowers, using your finger. Sprinkle the beads onto the adhesive. Allow the adhesive to dry.

10. Using the scissors, cut the corrugated cardboard to 5" x 7". Using pinking shears, cut the gold card stock ½" larger than the sunflower image on all sides.

11. Apply paper adhesive to the back of the first image and adhere it onto the gold card stock. Apply paper adhesive to the back of the gold card stock and adhere it onto the corrugated cardboard, using the photo for placement.

12. Using the makeup applicator, apply blue chalk all over a small scrap piece of ivory card stock.

13. Ink, print, and heat-emboss the phrase image onto the chalked ivory card stock. Using the pinking shears, cut it out. Apply paper adhesive to the back and adhere it onto a piece of gold card stock cut ¼" larger than the phrase. Apply paper adhesive to the back of the gold card stock and adhere it onto the corrugated cardboard.

14. Place your artwork in the frame.

section 3: *projects beyond the basics*

How do I stamp on fabric?

When I first began rubber stamping, I almost exclusively used paper. Later, someone encouraged me to try printing images onto fabric. I have been hooked ever since! Fabric stamping is fast and fun and opens up a world of exciting possibilities for you to explore. Baby clothes, sweatshirts, linens, sheets, lamp shades, denim jackets—all are waiting to be transformed by your rubber stamps!

What You Need to Get Started:

Apron
Cotton swab
Fabric paints:
   blue; light
   brown; medium
   brown; gold;
   red; yellow
Heavy cardboard
   or foamcore
   board
Kitchen towel:
   tan and white
   checked
Markers,
   permanent or
   fabric: blue;
   brown
Oven mitts: white
Paper towels
Sponge brush
Stamps: butter;
   checkerboard
   border; egg;
   measuring cup;
   mixer; mixing
   bowl; single
   check; wooden
   spoon

Baking Ensemble

Here's How:
Note: All fabric items follow the same instructions.

1. Lay the fabric item over a piece of heavy cardboard or foamcore board to protect the work surface and provide an even surface for stamping.

2. Dip the sponge brush into the blue paint, wiping off the excess. Apply the paint over the checkerboard border stamp so that the raised parts of the image are entirely covered. Let the paint sit on the stamp for one minute to form a base. Reapply the paint, removing any accumulated paint from the recesses of the image, using a cotton swab.

3. Print the image by placing the rubber die directly onto the fabric, applying even pressure without rocking or twisting the stamp. Lift the stamp off the fabric slowly so that any excess paint doesn't splatter.

4. Continue printing the image in this manner to create the border. When you reach the point where the border meets at a corner or other junction, use at least three layers of paper toweling to mask over the first part of the border so as to avoid overlapping the ends.

5. Using the method described in Steps 2–3, ink the largest image with the desired paint color. Print the image several times, randomly spaced, onto the fabric. Continue in this manner with the next largest image, and so on, finishing with the smallest image.

6. If desired, outline the printed butter image, using the blue marker, and the egg, using the brown marker. Outlining gives paler images more definition, particularly on a "busier" background.

7. Allow the fabric to dry overnight. Then, put the items in a clothes dryer set on medium heat for 30 minutes. The images are now permanently set and the fabric item can be washed and dried, following the manufacturer's instructions.

- To keep the garment from looking too busy, try not to use more than seven colors. Also, a little black used repeatedly throughout a busy design helps anchor the other colors and give them focus.

- Vary the sizes and shapes of the stamps so that the design has visual interest.

- To stamp on fabric with a detailed image, use fabric ink pads in the same way you would use a dye-based ink pad. Color the image with fabric marking pens.

Troubleshooting:

- Make certain you scrub the stamps well after each use (an old tooth-brush works) so dried paint doesn't build up and obscure the image.

- Because fabric paint is permanent, you will not be able to remove little unwanted lines. These lines can actually be considered an enhancement because they add to the hand-stamped look of the piece.

- If a portion of an image doesn't print when you stamp it, dip a cotton swab into the paint and tap it onto the fabric to fill in the area.

73

2

How do I create faux finishes with stamps?

What You Need to Get Started:

Acrylic paint:
  gold; ivory
Clock: wooden,
  arched
Clock face sticker
Clock movement
Paintbrush
Pigment ink pads:
  dark blue; grass
  green; mint
  green
Spray acrylic
  sealer: matte
  finish
Stamp set: faux
  marble (3 pieces)

Faux finishes are painting techniques applied to a particular material which create the "false" impression of another material. They represent a strong trend in decorating today. These effects can be achieved through stamping! Here I have used wood to make a "marble" clock. Look for stamps that will produce these elegant effects or experiment with some more abstract stamps, layering different colors on top of each other, and see what you can create.

Faux-marble Clock

Here's How:

1. Using the paintbrush, apply two coats of ivory paint onto the body of the clock. Apply two coats of gold paint onto the rim and base. Allow it to dry.

2. Ink the first stamp in the faux-marble stamp set, using the mint green ink pad. Randomly print the image onto the body of the clock.

3. Ink the second stamp, using the grass green ink pad. Randomly print the image onto the body of the clock.

4. Ink the third stamp, using the dark blue ink pad. Randomly print the image, although less densely, onto the body of the clock. Allow the ink to dry for 24 hours.

5. If desired, repeat the paint and ink applications on the back side of the clock.

6. Spray the entire clock with a coat of matte-finish sealer. Allow it to dry several hours.

7. Apply the clock face sticker and attach the clock movement, following the manufacturer's instructions.

Design Tips:

- There are some wonderful stamps available that simulate the look of wood graining, malachite stone, and leopard, giraffe, and zebra markings, to name a few.

- As you create projects using these stamps, experiment with materials to try simulating the texture of the desired finish as well. For example, a faux-leopard gift bag printed and embossed on suede paper would be a stunning visual and textural treat. A faux-malachite image stamped on slick jade green paper will fool the viewer's eyes and fingers!

3

How do I use stamps on terra-cotta?

What would make a lovelier gift than a beautiful flowering plant in a flower pot hand-stamped by you? Don't let the curved surface scare you—stamping on a pot is easier than you think!

Rose-covered Flower Pot

Here's How:
1. Using the sponge brush, apply two coats of ivory paint onto the outside of the flower pot. Allow it to dry.

2. Ink the stamp, using the black ink pad. Print the image onto the flower pot. (To stamp onto a curved surface, place one edge of the rubber die on the pot and roll the stamp over the pot until the entire image is printed.)

3. Continue in this manner, printing images around the pot, varying the heights of the rose.

4. Color the roses and leaves, using the paint pens and the photo opposite for placement. Allow the paint to dry.

5. If necessary, trace over the outlines of the roses, using the black paint pen.

6. Spray the entire pot with a coat of glossy-finish sealer. Allow the pot to dry several hours.

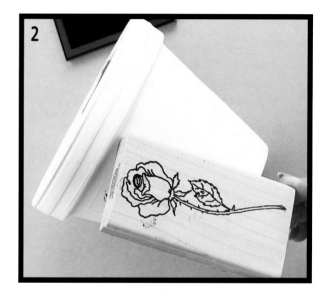

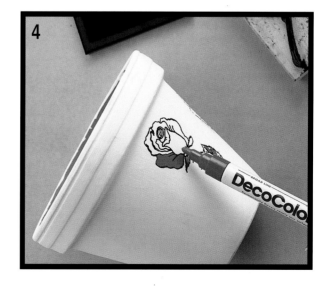

Design Tips:

- You can also stamp on un-painted ceramic pots. The terra-cotta color of the pot lends a wonderful, earthy look when coupled with ethnic or bold image stamps. Use crafter's ink that you heat-set or pigment ink that you heat-emboss. Apply a sealer to protect your work. Try combining stamped images with decorative elements like shells or beads.

- If you want to use a very large stamp to decorate your pot, try this method for getting a clear print of the image. Ink the stamp and place it, rubber die side up, on a flat surface. Holding the pot in both hands, place it on its side onto one end of the image and roll it across the stamp until the entire image has been printed.

77

4

How do I use stamps on wood?

Wood provides a wonderful hard surface for stamping. The interplay of the stamped image and the wood grain is appealing to the eye and the sense of touch. Craft stores carry a large assortment of small wooden pieces to choose from.

What You Need to Get Started:

Crafter's ink pads:
    black; brown;
    dark green;
    purple;
    turquoise
Heat gun
Permanent pen:
    black
Sandpaper: 150-
    grit
Spray acrylic
    sealer: matte
    finish
Stamps: small
    maple leaf;
    small oak leaf;
    small single
    check; small
    spruce leaf;
    small star
Tack cloth
Wooden salad
    bowl: medium
    size

Decorative Bowl

Here's How:
1. Using the sandpaper, sand the bowl smooth. Wipe dust from the bowl, using a tack cloth.

2. Ink the check stamp, using the turquoise ink pad. Print the image in three alternating rows along the inside rim of the bowl.

3. Ink the oak leaf stamp, using the brown ink pad. Print the image repeatedly underneath the checked border.

4. Ink the maple leaf stamp, using the purple ink pad. Ink the star stamp, using the black ink pad. Print the images alternately, underneath the oak leaves.

5. Ink the spruce leaf stamp, using the dark green ink pad. Print the image onto the center of the bowl, over-lapping the leaves to form a star pattern, using the photo opposite for placement.

6. Ink the check stamp, using the turquoise ink pad. Print the image in three alternating rows along the outside rim of the bowl.

7. Draw lines along the edge of the bowl, using the black pen.

8. Hold the heat gun about 5" away from a section of the bowl for about 2½ minutes, taking care not to scorch the bowl. Continue until each section has set.

9. Spray the entire bowl with a coat of matte-finish sealer. Allow it to dry several hours.

Note: The bowl is for decorative purposes only.

Design Tips:
•   This project demonstrates stamp-ing on natural, unstained wood. When stamping on darker, stained wood, use bold-faced stamps with pigment ink and heat-emboss the stamped images so that they stand out from the background.

•   If you like the look of a colored bowl with the wood grain show-ing through, you can easily achieve this effect. Dilute a desired color of acrylic paint with a little water, brush it on with a sponge brush or makeup sponge, and wipe the excess off with a paper towel. Allow the wooden piece to dry and proceed with your stamping.

How do I use foam stamps?

What You Need to Get Started:

Acrylic paints:
light blue;
seafoam green;
peach; yellow
Clothespins
Craft adhesive
Fabric trim:
peach (1 yd.)
Foam stamp set:
posy
Lamp base:
coordinating
Lamp shade kit:
small
Paper: scraps (to
test the images)
Permanent fine-
tipped pen:
black
Sponge brush
Spray acrylic
sealer: matte
finish

Relatively new to the stamp field, foam stamps are an excellent choice for home decorating projects. They are deeply etched, making it easy to achieve a clean printing, and they grip surfaces like walls and furniture very nicely.

Floral Lamp Shade

Here's How:
1. Lay the lamp shade material flat on a clean work surface.

2. Beginning with the large posy stamp, load the sponge brush with the light blue paint, removing any excess paint. Ink the stamp by tapping the sponge brush over the image until it is covered, but not runny with paint.

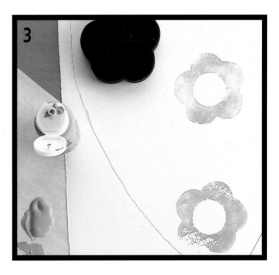

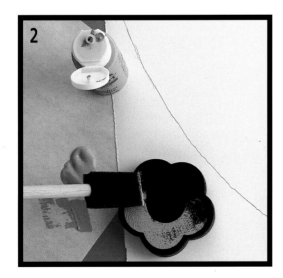

3. Test-print the image by pressing the stamp onto a piece of scrap paper and lifting it straight off. Adjust the amount of paint as needed and print the image onto the lamp shade.

4. Load the sponge brush with the yellow paint in the same manner as in Step 2 and ink the small posy stamp. Print the image onto the lamp shade. Repeat several times so that the small posies loosely circle the large posies.

5. Using the mask provided in the stamp set for the large posy, cover the large printed posy. Load the sponge brush with the seafoam green paint and ink the leaf stamp. Print the image onto the lamp shade to the side of the masked posy. Repeat this process with the smaller printed posy images and smaller leaf stamp.

6. Continue stamping the lamp shade in this manner until the pattern is completed.

7. Load the sponge brush with the peach paint and ink the stamps to be used for the centers of the flowers. Print the images for all the flower centers. Allow all paint to dry several hours.

8. Using the black pen, outline the flowers and leaves with a small "stitch" line.

9. Spray the lamp shade with a coat of matte-finish sealer. Allow it to dry for several hours.

10. Apply adhesive along one side edge of the shade and adhere the two edges of the shade together. Secure the edges, using the clothespins. Allow the adhesive to dry.

11. Apply adhesive along the top and bottom edge of the shade and adhere the fabric trim onto the shade. Allow the adhesive to dry.

12. Assemble the lamp shade, frame, and base, following the manufacturer's instructions.

How do I use stamps to emboss velvet?

Iron and ironing board
Satin liner fabric: blue, 46" x 12"
Sewing machine or fabric glue
Silk fringe trim: black (⅓ yd.)
Spray bottle (for misting)
Stamps: clam shell; conch shell; star fish
Velvet fabric: rayon/silk, midnight blue, 46" x 12" (avoid cotton velvet, polyester velvet, or velveteen)

Have you noticed the elegant embossed velvet wearables and home accessories being featured in all of the trendy stores lately? They are so rich looking, but the problem is they are frequently accompanied by a rich price tag! However, you do not need to break the bank to add embossed velvet to your life. Rubber stamps can create distinctive and permanent impressions in velvet. Whether or not you sew, there are all sorts of beautiful things you can create with bold faced stamps and velvet.

Seashell Velvet Scarf

Here's How:
Note: No ink is required for this project. Dry clean all velvet garments.

1. Lay a stamp, rubber die side up, on the ironing board. Beginning at one end of the velvet fabric, place it, nap side down, over the stamp where you want the impression to be made. The wrong side of the fabric should be facing you.

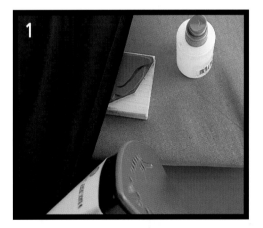

2. Set the iron to "wool" setting with no steam. Lightly mist the back side of the fabric with water so that it is slightly damp. Place the iron onto the fabric and press, without wiggling the iron, for about 20 seconds. Lift the iron, turn it one quarter to the right or left, and press again for five seconds to eliminate any unpressed circles that may have resulted from the iron's steam circles.

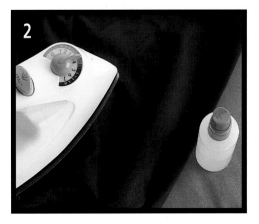

Design Tips:

- Velvet embossing works best with bold-faced stamps. Avoid highly detailed images. The velvet is too thick to be able to pick up fine lines.

- Random placement of images works best with velvet embossing since it is nearly impossible to line up images accurately.

- Not a seamstress? You don't have to be. There are many ways you can use embossed velvet without sewing. Try adding a piece of embossed velvet inside a picture frame card or box. Embossed velvet looks wonderful adhered to a scrapbook cover. Look in stores for plain velvet dresses, shirts, and purses that you can embellish with your own designer touch!

Reposition the fabric over the stamp and repeat this process until the entire piece of velvet is embossed.

3. Sew or glue the velvet to its liner. Sew or glue silk fringe trim onto each short end.

4. Steam seams down so that they lay relatively flat. Do not try to iron the seams as this will leave an unwanted impression in the velvet.

project 7

How do I create jewelry with stamps?

My favorite material for rubber stamped jewelry is shrink plastic. Stamp on the shrink plastic, cut out the images, and watch them shrink down to make adorable charms. Combine the shrink art you have created with coordinating beads or charms and your friends will wonder which trendy boutique you've been shopping in!

What You Need to Get Started:

Charms: small
star (2)
Colored pencils:
light blue;
light green;
rose; yellow
Crafter's ink pad:
black
Instant adhesive
Earring backs (2)
Heat gun (or
toaster oven)
Hole punch: ¼"
Jump rings (2)
Paper: scrap
Permanent pen:
gold
Sandpaper:
320-400 grit
Scissors
Shrink plastic:
opaque
(2 sheets)
Stamp positioner
Stamp: moon

Moon & Stars Earrings

Here's How:

1. Lightly sand the shrink plastic, using the sandpaper, following the manufacturer's instructions.

2. Ink the moon stamp, using the black ink pad. Print the image onto scrap paper. Place the shrink plastic over the image and color the plastic, using the outline from underneath and the photo opposite for placement. Repeat this process for the second earring.

3. Ink the stamp, using the black ink pad. Using the stamp positioner, line up the stamp directly over each scrap paper image. Print the image onto each colored image on the shrink plastic.

4. Using the scissors, cut out the images. Be careful not to smudge the ink as it is not permanent until it is heated.

5. Using the hole punch, punch a hole at the bottom edge of each image.

6. Direct the heat gun at the stamped image until it begins to shrink. It will curl up, contort, and then flatten out.

Once the image is flat and has finished shrinking, turn off the heat gun. (Alternatively, bake the images in a toaster oven at 300° for about three minutes.) It is amazing to see how much your image shrinks. Compare it to the image shown at actual size below.

Image shown actual size.

7. Outline the shrunken images, using the gold pen. Allow the images to dry for about 30 minutes.

8. Insert a jump ring through each hole and thread on a small star charm before closing the jump ring. Apply instant adhesive to two earring backs and adhere one onto the center back of each image to finish the earrings.

Troubleshooting:

- The shrunken images may seem to have changed shape from the original. Horizontally and vertically positioned images shrink slightly differently. If you have laid out an image horizontally and are un- happy with its shrunken form, stamp it vertically and see if you are happier with the results.

- You may be concerned how the finished product will look because the colored pencils do not color evenly on the plastic. You're in luck! As the plastic shrinks, the colors compress and intensify, making this a very forgiving process.

Design Tips:

- Shrink plastic comes in 8½" x 11" sheets in black, clear, opaque, and white. If you use ink to color the image, you must use permanent ink or crafter's ink to perma- nently set the color on shrink plastic. All other inks will smear. Colored pencils or acrylic paints are also excellent choices for color- ing images. Choose large images because they will shrink to half their size.

- You may stamp the image directly onto the shrink plastic with permanent ink. However, make certain the image is completely dry before coloring it. You can also stamp the images you want onto copy paper and then hand-feed the shrink plastic through the copy machine. The images will print nicely onto the shrink plastic. Make certain you have sanded the shrink plastic before you copy the images onto it. Also, only feed shrink plastic through a copy machine that has been turned on recently so that it is not too warm.

- There are many ways to make jewelry using rubber stamps. Heavy paper, poly- mer clay, and paper clay are some other materials that stamp beautifully and can be turned into jewelry.

project 8

How do I use stamps with decorative foil?

What you Need to Get Started:

Card stock:
    glossy red
Foil: variegated
    gold
Foil adhesive
Paintbrush or
    sponge brush
Paper adhesive
Scissors
Spray acrylic
    sealer: glossy
    finish
Spray paint:
    glossy black
Stamp: fan
Wooden picture
    frame

Decorative foils add elegance to any project and are easy to use with stamps. Foils come in many colors and in variegated tones and patterns. Instead of using ink on the stamp, you can apply foil adhesive to it. Stamp the image, let the adhesive dry, and apply the foils. It is that easy!

Asian Fan Picture Frame

Here's How:

1. Spray the frame with the black spray paint in a well-ventilated area. Allow it to dry. Apply a second coat if necessary.

2. Spray the frame with a coat of glossy-finish sealer in a well-ventilated area. Allow it to dry.

3. Using the paintbrush or sponge brush, apply a small amount of the foil adhesive all over the stamp. Print the image onto the card stock. Allow it to dry for about 10 minutes (until the adhesive feels tacky). Repeat this process to create four images. Wash the stamp to clean off the adhesive.

4. Take a small amount of foil in your fingers and lay it on top of each printed image. Apply enough foil so that the entire image is covered. Rub off the foil that is not stuck to the adhesive. Using the scissors, cut out the images, leaving a small border of the card stock.

5. Apply paper adhesive to the back of the cut-out images. Adhere one image onto each corner of the frame.

6. Cut out a small piece of card stock for the opening of the frame. Apply adhesive to the back of the art to be framed and adhere it onto the center of the card stock.

Troubleshooting:
• If the details of the image are not pronounced when stamped, try using a thinner coat of the foil adhesive.

9

How do I use stamps on glass and porcelain?

There is no need to settle for ordinary dishes! Decorate your dishware and customize it for any table setting, using rubber stamps and porcelain paint. Go ahead and stamp your glassware to match—it is simple with rubber stamps. All pieces will be dishwasher and microwave safe. *

Confetti Dinnerware

* While these paints are completely nontoxic, they are not intended for use on surfaces that come into direct contact with food or drink. For example, avoid painting on the rims of mugs and glasses.

Here's How:
1. Prepare the surface, using the conditioner provided in the paint kit, following the manufacturer's instructions.

2. For both the polka-dot and the single check images, load a makeup sponge, using the first paint color. Apply the paint over the stamp, so the image is lightly covered. Gently print the image onto the rim of the plate.

3. First print the polka-dots, using one paint color, then fill in the balance of the plate rim with polka-dots, using the other three paint colors alternately.

4. Print the checks, using the photo opposite for placement. Allow the porcelain pieces to dry for at least one hour.

5. If desired, apply the glossy sealer provided in the kit, using the paintbrush. Clean the paintbrush with water.

Design Tip:
• Check flea markets, thrift shops, and yard sales for inexpensive, unadorned porcelain pieces. Craft stores also sell a variety of porcelain pieces that work beautifully—including plain white tiles. Several woodenware companies make shelves, tables, trays, trivets, and clocks that are made to encase the tiles—you simply glue them into place. In no time at all you can make an attractive and functional decorated item for your home.

section 4: *gallery*

Marie P. Dubois (pictured left) has worked for Magenta since 1991. She also studies art, design, and textile printing at the Montreal Center of Design (a Canadian college of design and textile printing), where she is developing her artistic talent and amazing sense of colors. As a result, her vision and her work as a stamp artist are very much influenced by her mastery of color and design combinations.

Magenta is a Canadian rubber stamp manufacturer well known for its unique artistic designs and detailed engravings. Magenta artists have developed very effective techniques that make the company one of the leaders in the industry. Their goal is to make rubber stamping a recognized part of visual art.

designed by Marie P. Dubois

designed by Marie P. Dubois

designed by Marie P. Dubois

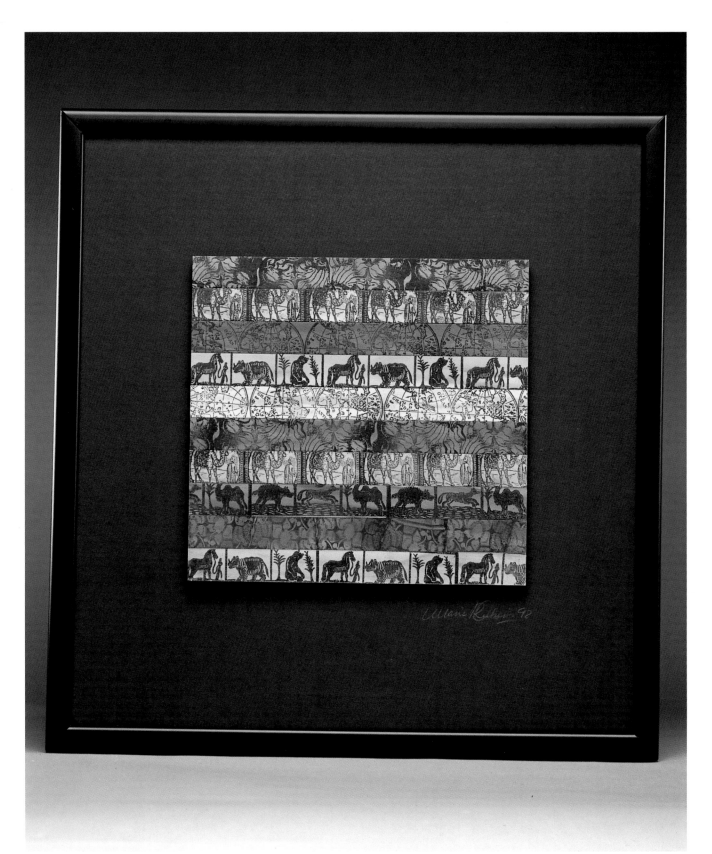

designed by Marie P. Dubois

93

designed by Cynthia Elmore

Cynthia Elmore, well-known illustrator and designer, has been associated for over 10 years with Personal Stamp Exchange, a leader in the rubber stamping industry. Her beautifully detailed designs are familiar to rubber stamp aficionados worldwide.

Cynthia's lifelong work as an artist began with her formal education at the University of North Carolina, continuing to a professional career first in design and fabrication of stained glass and sand-blasted glass, then in commercial art. Most recently, Cynthia has focused her talents on rubber stamp design, craft project design, and painting in water mediums. Her contributions have played an important role in creating the elegant and classic look for which Personal Stamp Exchange is known.

designed by Cynthia Elmore

Dee Gruenig is recognized as a master of innovation when it comes to adapting stamping accessories to create original stamping effects.

In 1989, Dee became the first to demonstrate rubber stamping to a television audience. She has since appeared numerous times on popular television craft shows. She has also represented various product manufacturers and retailers.

As a teacher, Dee has taught approximately 30,000 students personally and many more by means of four videos and four books about the craft. Additionally, she teaches rubber stamping to art and craft instructors of the United States Army in the U.S. and abroad.

Dee has her own line of stamps and owns and operates Posh Impressions, which is made up of two retail stores. She has served on two major industry related advisory boards and is currently serving on the Hobby Industry Association (HIA) Board of Directors.

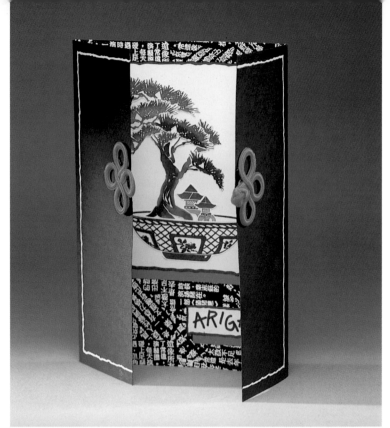

designed by Dee Gruenig

designed by Dee Gruenig

You are invited to an Open House
in celebration of

Mike and Rita Johnson's
Silver Wedding Anniversary

Please join us on
Sunday, May 17th
from 1:00 to 5:00 at
36 South Portola
South Laguna

Todd and Paula Williams
Dave and Sue DePierro

Please RSVP by May 11th
(714) 499-5339

Robert Young

designed by Dee Gruenig

designed by Deb Highfill

Deb Highfill has been a valuable member of the marketing team at Uptown Rubber Stamps™ for the past four years, creating hand-stamped art for the company's catalogs, how-to books, and demo boards. Deb's favorite mediums are colored pencil and watercolor.

Uptown Rubber Stamps™ is a wholesale manufacturer of rubber stamps and a distributor of stamping accessories. Their goal is to provide their customers with fun new designs and charming, classic images that consumers are looking for. Their collection includes Boyds Bears™ & Friends, Holly Pond Hill®, Sandi Gore Evans, David Walker, and others. Uptown designs can be found in rubber stamp and gift stores.

designed by Deb Highfill

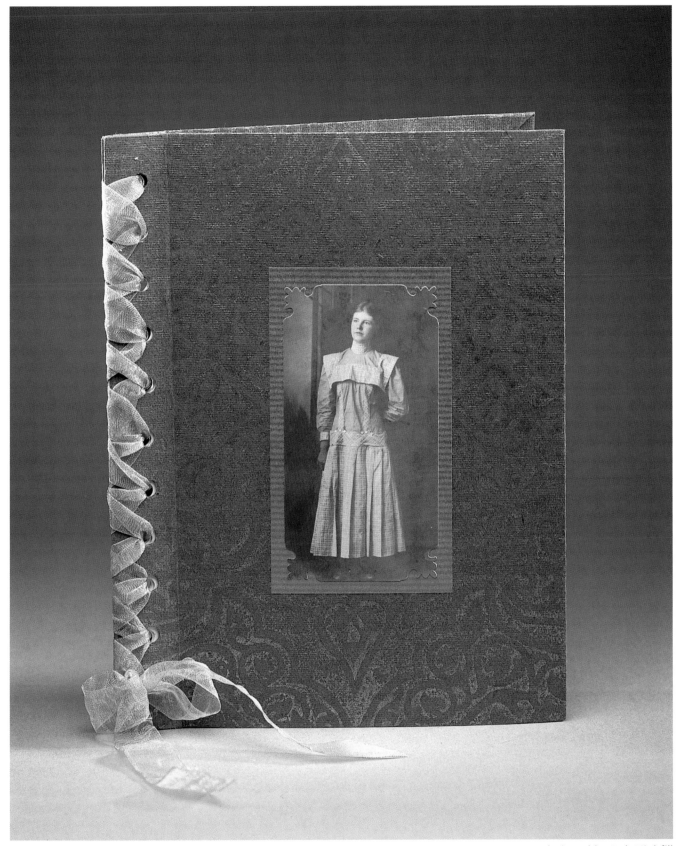

designed by Deb Highfill

Sherrill Kahn taught Fine Arts for 30 years in the Los Angeles Unified School District in California, emphasizing drawing, painting, and design. She has taught for a variety of quilt and crafts guilds throughout the United States. She has also taught workshops for fabric, rubber stamp, craft, and bead stores.

With her husband Joel, she started her own rubber stamp company called Impress Me. Their unique designs are all hand-drawn originals. Sherrill has had her designs published in magazines and books relating to fiber arts and rubber stamping. She loves to teach and enjoys sharing the unique and creative techniques that she has discovered through constant experimentation.

designed by Sherill Kahn

designed by Sherill Kahn

designed by Sherill Kahn

Impress Me rubber stamps are very deeply etched. The hand-drawn, original designs can be used on a variety of surfaces and in projects ranging from stamping on cloth, to stamping on paper and curved surfaces. The stamps are heavy and unmounted, providing for ease of use and cleaning. Additionally, the stamps lend themselves beautifully to border designs and repeat patterns. Many of the stamps are based upon petroglyphs and ethnic designs. Rubber stampers, quilt makers, creative book artists, wearables artists, cloth doll makers, ceramists, polyform clay artists, shrink art users, card makers, laminators, mail artists, hand-made paper artists, and jewelry makers discover a new horizon using these unique rubber stamps in their finished projects.

Kathy Lewis never met a rubber stamp she didn't like. Consequently, stamps have taken over her life—and her house. Her collection consists of more that 35,000 stamps and is growing strong.

Kathy is driven to justify her very large acquisition by teaching workshops on rubber stamping when she is not teaching Mathematics at California State University Fullerton. Initially, she was an art major, but she decided to switch to math, thinking it would offer better job security. She is thankful that she loves doing both as what one doesn't provide, the other offers and vice versa.

Kathy has been teaching stamping workshops for 12 years. She works in cooperation with Debra Valoff and her company, Rubbermoon Stamps, crafting delightful works of art. Kathy credits her wonderful husband and three children who "tolerate" her hobby and the accompanying smell of rubber in their house.

designed by Kathy Lewis

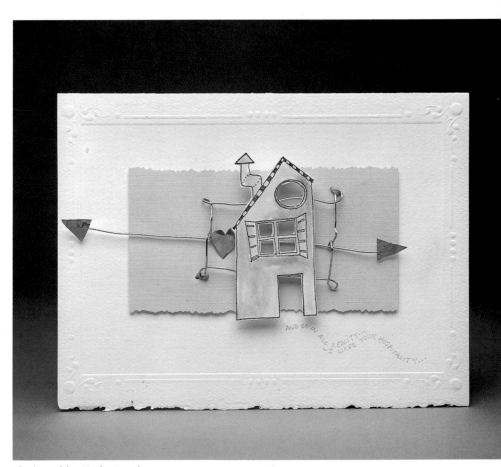

designed by Kathy Lewis

101

Kevin Nakagawa began his rubber stamp design career in 1987, working for Kathie Okamoto at A Stamp in the Hand Co.™. There, he designed several series of images including the "Nature Series" which became the precursor of his own line of unique stamps.

Kevin started Stampscapes® in 1993 based on the idea of combining, merging, and overlapping individual interchangeable nature elements to form seamless scenes. Currently, his line consists of more than 200 images that are primarily available to wholesale buyers and by mail order catalog.

access can view hundreds of samples created by Kevin and other stamping artists who have worked Stampscapes® images into their artwork.

Aside from time spent designing, he keeps himself busy posting updates on his website at "stampscapes.com" where anyone with internet

Kevin frequently attends retail stamping conventions and occasionally teaches workshops around the United States.

designed by Kevin Nakagawa

designed by Kevin Nakagawa

designed by Kevin Nakagawa

designed by Kevin Nakagawa

designed by Kevin Nakagawa

Debra Valoff is a stamp artist who loves all forms of paper arts. Her stamped work usually involves paper constructions and colored pencils.

As a young wife and mother living in Fresno, California, Debra taught quilting and dollmaking at several local quilt shops. It was in her quilting that she developed her use of color.

Rubber stamping has been part of Debra's life since the time that her two sons were small and the family made their own Christmas and Valentine's Day cards. In late 1993 she started her own company called Rubbermoon Stamps.

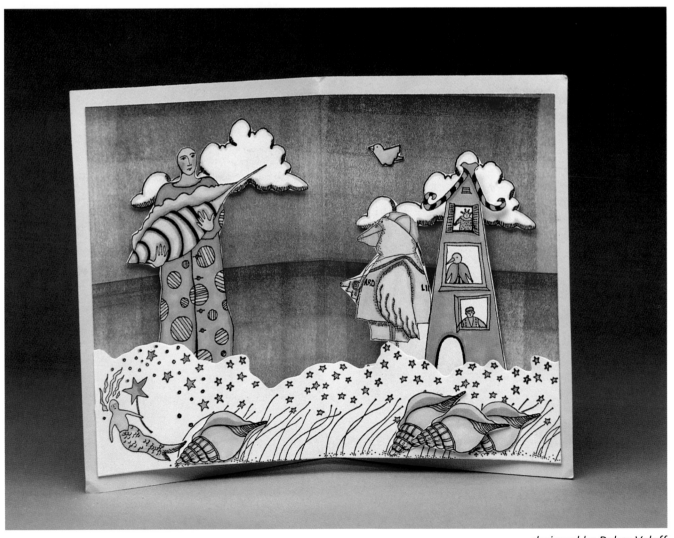

designed by Debra Valoff

105

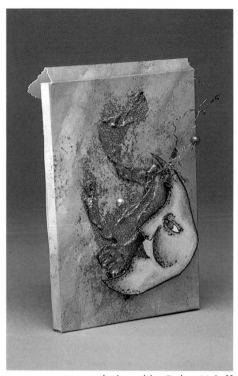

designed by Debra Valoff

designed by Debra Valoff

These days, Debra can be seen mostly in her garage, indexing wood, and occasionally in Seattle, teaching stamping classes.

She currently resides in northern Idaho with her husband, two sons, one daughter-in-law, two dogs, and a rubber stamp company (fortunately, not all under one roof).

designed by Debra Valoff

Nationally known rubber stamper **Suze Weinberg** has been designing and creating with rubber stamps for over 15 years. Suze, a past president of Jersey Shore Calligraphers' Guild, has been a professional calligrapher for 16 years and owns and operates her own agency, The Suze Weinberg Design Studio, Inc., in Howell, New Jersey. Her calligraphic and stamped work has been published in the *Speedball Textbook, The Greeting Card Design Book,* The Rubber Stamper Magazine, RubberStampMadness, National Stampagraphic, VAMP Stamp News, Calligraphy Review, and her own calligraphy book titled *Do It Yourself Calligraphy.*

Suze teaches rubber stamp classes for stamp stores, clubs, and conventions, in addition to calligraphy workshops for guilds and conferences, in the United States and abroad. In January 1997, Suze began writing a question and answer column called "Schmooze with Suze" for The Rubber Stamper Magazine. Her first video, "Ultimate Enamels," premiered in 1998.

Suze has also developed several stamping products and is regarded as a consultant in the rubber stamp industry.

She and her husband, Lenny, a marine engineer, have been married for 35 years. They have three children and three grandchildren.

designed by Suze Weinberg

designed by Suze Weinberg

designed by Suze Weinberg

designed by Suze Weinberg

actual products used

Angel Ornaments, page 26
Colored pencils by Spectracolor:
canary yellow; crimson lake; grass
green; light salmon
Dual-tipped markers by Tombow: hunter
green #249; red #845; tan #990;
yellow #55
Folk art angel stamp by Carmen's
Veranda
Spray acrylic sealer by Krylon: matte
finish

Asian Fan Picture Frame, page 86
Crane and sun stamp by Curtis Uyeda
Fan stamp by Hot Potatoes
Foil adhesive by Magic Leaf
Spray acrylic sealer by High-Shine
Spray paint by Krylon: black
Variegated foil by Magic Leaf
10" x 10" picture frame by Walnut
Hollow

Baking Ensemble, page 72
Checkerboard stamp by Hot Potatoes
All other stamps by Great American
Stamp Store
Fabric paints by Deka: blueberry; brown;
crimson; desert yellow; light brown;
mission gold
Fine point permanent markers by
Sharpie: blue; brown

Bear Claw Stationery Set, page 62
Checkerboard heart stamp by That's All
She Stamped
Embossing powder by Great American
Stamp Store: verdigris
Embossing powder by Judi-Kins: jasper
Ornamental square stamp by Rubber
Stampede

Birdhouse Greeting Card, page 48
Birdhouse stamp by Imaginations
Daisy stamp by Embossing Arts
Watercolors—Flowers: orange; yellow
Watercolors—Leaves: medium green
Watercolors—Larger birdhouse: brown;
medium blue; red; yellow
Watercolors—Smaller birdhouse: brown;
green; medium blue; orange; purple;
yellow

Bordered Picture Frame Card, page 52
Colored pencils by Spectracolor:
canary yellow; crimson red; green;
light blue; pink

Heart frame card by All Night Media
Ink pad by Vivid: black
Posy stamp by Printworks
Stamp positioner by Stampa Barbara

Celestial Photo Album, page 64
Angel hair by Kurt S. Adler (Christmas
decoration)
Checkerboard star stamp by Great
American Stamp Store
Dotted star stamp by Paper Source
Sun stamp by Stamp Francisco
8" x 8" photo album by Michael Roger
Press, Inc.

Colorful Bookmark, page 30
Bookmark and green tassel by All
Night Media
Brush art markers by Marvy: green #98;
magenta #20; purple #8; red #65
Raspberry stamp by Zim Prints

Confetti Dinnerware, page 88
Air-Dry PermEnamel Shimmers Starter
Kit by Delta: emerald green #45112;
golden glow #45111; purple pizzazz
#45113; raspberry sherbet #45109
PermEnamel Surface Conditioner by
Delta
Single check stamp by Printworks
Small polka dot stamp by Printworks

Decorative Bowl, page 78
Crafter's pigment ink pads by Colorbox:
black; brown; dark green; purple;
turquoise
Maple leaf stamp by Personal Stamp
Exchange
Single check stamp by Printworks
Spray acrylic sealer by Krylon: matte
finish
Spruce leaf stamp by All Night Media
Star and oak leaf stamp by unknown
designer

Decorative Journal, page 34
Beach scene stamp by Burton Morris
Dual-tipped markers by Tombow: light
aqua #351; pink #821; red #845;
royal blue #452; tan #912; yellow
#55
Pigment ink pad by Colorbox: royal
blue #15015

Heat-embossed Picture Matte, page 36
Birch leaf stamp by Stamp Francisco

Embossing ink pad by Top Boss: clear
Embossing powder by The Herbarium:
antique gold
Embossing powders by Personal Stamp
Exchange: claret; cobalt; copper
Fern stamp by Fred Mullett
Oak leaf stamp by Rubber Stampede
Set of tiny leaf stamps by All Night
Media
Small maple leaf stamp by Personal
Stamp Exchange

Faux-marble Clock, page 74
Acrylic paints by Delta Ceramcoat: gold;
ivory
Clock movement for ¾"-thick clock face
by Walnut Hollow
Marble texture cube #TCOI by
Stampendous
Medium arched clock by Walnut Hollow
Pigment ink pads by Colorbox: green
#15021; mint #15040; royal blue
#15018
Roman numerals clock face by Walnut
Hollow
Spray acrylic sealer by Krylon: matte
finish
Stamps by Stampendous

Floral Lamp Shade, page 80
Accent paints by Koh-I-noor: devonshire
cream #2312; peaches n' cream
#2420
"Cool Shades" lamp shade kit by Kiti
Folk Art paints by Plaid: baby blue
#442; robin's egg #915
Permanent pen by Micron: #005
Posy Stamp Set Designer Printblocks,
"Fresh Flowers" #PB003 by
Printworks
Spray acrylic sealer by Krylon: matte
finish

Framed Sunflowers, page 68
Beads by Beedz: gold
Dual-tipped marker by Tombow: black
Embossing pens by Marvy: gold #43;
dark green #4; light green #11;
orange #7; yellow #5
Ink pad by Colorbox: black
"Sunflower" phrase stamp by
Printworks
Sunflower stamp by Print Kraft:
#21001 M

Gift Bags for New Babies, page 56
Archival ink pad by Ranger: coffee
Colored pencils by Spectracolor: brown
    #1438; dark purple #1431; dark
    yellow #1436; light blue #1433;
    pink #1427; silver gray #1428
Large shoe stamp by Stampendous
Pigma Pen by Micron: brown
Remaining stamps by Effie Glitzfinger
Star stamp by Dream a Little
Watercolor pencils by Derwent:
    light blue; light brown
"Yippee" phrase stamp by Hero Arts

Halloween Party Ideas, page 66
Brush art markers by Marvy: black #1;
    brown #54; dark orange #49; grass
    green #48; light brown #30; light
    gray #51; pink #47; purple #31; sky
    blue #75; yellow #5
Pigment ink pad by Colorbox: black
Candy corn, ghost, gravestone, pumpkin,
    spider, "Trick or Treat" phrase, and
    "You're Invited" phrase stamps by
    Azadi Earle
Witch stamp by That's All She Stamped

Moon & Stars Earrings, page 84
Calligraphy pen by Marvy Uchida: gold
Colored pencils by Spectracolor: light
    blue #1433; light green #1447; rose
    #1424; yellow #1423
Crafter's pigment ink pad by Colorbox:
    black
Instant adhesive by Krazy Glue
Moon and stars stamp by Rubber
    Moon

Plant Markers, page 54
Brush art markers by Marvy: coral #49;
    dark green #4; dark purple #8; light
    blue #41; light green #48; medium
    green #97; medium purple #78;
    pink #9; red #2; yellow #5
Daisy, hydrangea, rose, and tulip stamps
    by Posh Impressions
Dual-tipped marker by Tombow: black
Embossing markers by Marvy
    Matchables: dark green; red

Rainbow Star Card, page 32
Brush art markers by Marvy: aqua #53;
    magenta #20; orange #49; pink #9;
    red #2;
Dye-based ink pad by Vivid: black
Eight point star stamp by Hot Potatoes
"The Stars Exist That We Might Know
    How High Our Dreams Can Soar"
    phrase stamp by Great American
    Stamp Store

Recipe Cards, page 42
Baked Apple Card:
Apple stamp by All Night Media
Brush art markers by Marvy: dark green
    #98; green #48; red #89; yellow #5

Blueberry Muffin Card:
Brush art markers by Marvy: brown
    #90; cranberry #65; dark blue #3;
    royal blue #10
Muffin stamp by Paper Garden

Hearty Autumn Soup Card:
Brush art markers by Marvy: cinnamon
    #13; dark orange #88; pea green
    #96
Leaf stamp by Rubber Stampede
Rainbow ink pad by Ranger's Big and
    Juicy Pads: spice

Heavenly Brickle Bar Card:
Angels stamp by Stamp Francisco
Brush art markers by Marvy: aqua
    #104; royal blue #10; seafoam
    green #71

Tropical Fruit Salsa Card:
Brush art markers by Marvy: green #48;
    hot pink #9; orange #49; yellow #5
Palm tree stamp by Hot Potatoes
Rainbow ink pad by Ranger's Big and
    Juicy Pads: tutti frutti

Rose-covered Flower Pot, page 76
Acrylic paint by Delta Ceramcoat: ivory
Paint pens by Marvy: black; dark green;
    dark pink; light pink; red
Rose stamp by Art Gone Wild
Spray acrylic sealer by Krylon: glossy
    finish
8" terra-cotta pot

Scrapbook Page, page 38
Alphabet stickers by Frances Meyer, Inc.
Beach chair stamp by Printworks
Brush art markers by Marvy—Cloud
    Frame: black #1; lavender #62;
    light blue #41; light pink #57;
    peach #16
Brush art markers by Marvy—Deckle-
    edged Frame: medium blue #10;
    sky blue #41; tan #44; yellow #5
Brush art markers by Marvy—Postage
    Frame: dark pink #9; dark purple
    #8; light pink #57; light purple #62
Brush art markers by Marvy—Scroll
    Frame: dark pink #9; yellow #5
Cloud stamp by Distinked Impressions
Sand dunes and water stamps by Posh
    Impressions

School of fish stamp by Hampton Art
    Stamp
Scroll frame stamp by Judi-kins
Sea horse stamp by Fred B. Mullett
Pail, sand castle, and shovel stamps by
    Great American Stamp Store
Postage frame stamp by
    Stampacadabra
Umbrella stamp by Remarkable!

Seashell Velvet Scarf, page 82
All stamps by Hot Potatoes

Simple Gift Tag, page 24
Brush art marker by Marvy: red #89
Girl holding heart stamp by The Paper
    Garden

Travel Photo Journal, page 46
"Bon voyage!" phrase stamp by Magenta
Dye-based ink pads by Adirondack:
    bottle; cranberry
Dye-based ink pads by Vivid: black;
    plum; ultramarine
Faux Cairo, compass, Java, New York,
    San Francisco travel stamps by
    Stamp Francisco
Faux Ireland and Italy postage stamps
    by Ivory Coast
Photo frame stamp by Stampa Barbara

Video Tape Cover, page 58
Alphabet, grass, rose, and water stamps
    by Rubber Stampede
Bear and hotdog stamps by Art Gone
    Wild
Brush art markers by Marvy: blue green
    #14; grass green #37; light green
    #70
Campfire stamp by Love You to Bits
Colored pencils by Spectracolor: cocoa
    #1428; dark gray #1440; dark
    yellow #1423; light blue #1433;
    light yellow #1448; lime green
    #1422; medium brown #1416;
    orange #1402; pink #1427
Pegasus stamp by Personal Stamp
    Exchange
Rocks stamp by Art Impressions
Small cloud stamp by Hero Arts
Television stamp by Burton Morris
Trees stamp by Good Good the
    Elephant
Water-skier stamp by Stampa Barbara

metric equivalency chart

mm–millimetres   cm–centimetres
inches to millimetres and centimetres

inches	mm	cm	inches	cm	inches	cm	inches	cm
1/8	3	0.3	6	15.2	21	53.3	36	91.4
1/4	6	0.6	7	17.8	22	55.9	37	94.0
3/8	10	1.0	8	20.3	23	58.4	38	96.5
1/2	13	1.3	9	22.9	24	61.0	39	99.1
5/8	16	1.6	10	25.4	25	63.5	40	101.6
3/4	19	1.9	11	27.9	26	66.0	41	104.1
7/8	22	2.2	12	30.5	27	68.6	42	106.7
1	25	2.5	13	33.0	28	71.1	43	109.2
1 1/4	32	3.2	14	35.6	29	73.7	44	111.8
1 1/2	38	3.8	15	38.1	30	76.2	45	114.3
1 3/4	44	4.4	16	40.6	31	78.7	46	116.8
2	51	5.1	17	43.2	32	81.3	47	119.4
3	76	7.6	18	45.7	33	83.8	48	121.9
4	102	10.2	19	48.3	34	86.4	49	124.5
5	127	12.7	20	50.8	35	88.9	50	127.0

index